THE
COUNTRY BOOK
OF
HERBS
&
SPICES

THE
COUNTRY BOOK
OF
HERBS
&
SPICES

JOANNA SHEEN

PHOTOGRAPHY BY
LIZZIE ORME

SMITHMARK

*I would like to dedicate this book to the new little herb
in our garden, Emily Constance, who I am sure will bring us all as
much joy and happiness as her older sister has done.*

First published in Great Britain in 1993 by
Anaya Publishers Ltd, London

Text copyright © Joanna Sheen 1993
Photography and illustrations copyright © Anaya Publishers 1993

Managing Editor Jane Struthers
Design Peartree Design Associates
Photography Lizzie Orme
Styling and Backgrounds Linda Barker
Home Economist Meg Jansz
Illustrations Richard Lowther and Lynne Robinson

This edition published in 1994 by SMITHMARK Publishers Inc.,
16 East 32nd Street, New York, NY 10016.

SMITHMARK books are available for bulk purchase for sales
promotion and premium use. For details write or call the
manager of special sales, SMITHMARK Publishers Inc.,
16 East 32nd Street, New York, NY 10016; (212) 532-6600.

Produced by Anaya Publishers Ltd., 3rd Floor, Strode House,
44–50 Osnaburgh Street, London NW1 3ND.

ISBN 0–8317–1159–0

Printed in Italy

10 9 8 7 6 5 4 3 2 1

CONTENTS

IMPORTANT

Use only one set of measurements. Measurements are given in metric and imperial, plus American cups, where appropriate, but the conversions are not always exact and the quantities given are not interchangeable.

Essential oils are powerful liquids and should not be used to treat serious or chronic medical conditions without consulting a professional and qualified aromatherapist. Never apply the essential oils neat to your skin, and test a patch of skin for allergic reactions before using any oil. If you are receiving any course of medical treatment do not take any herbal remedies without first seeking professional advice.

All essential oils should be treated with care and respect. The following are not suitable for use during pregnancy: angelica, basil, bay, clary sage, cumin, fennel, lovage, juniper, marjoram, tarragon, thyme. Diabetics should avoid using rosemary and epileptics should not use angelica.

This book is only intended for guidance and should not be used as a medical reference book or self-treatment manual.

INTRODUCTION

♣

Herbs and spices have been used both medicinally and in the kitchen for many thousands of years and their versatility is quite amazing. While learning gradually over the years about the various properties of plants, seeds, roots and flowers which can all be harnessed and put to good use in our lives, I have never stopped marvelling at the brilliant wonders of the natural world.

Although fashions in fresh and dried flowers may come and go, I hope the use of herbs and spices in floral decorations will remain popular for a long time. They add such special fragrances and colours to arrangements and can turn a very simple display into something much more special.

It is worth discovering some of the uses for herbal and spicy essential oils as they can sometimes offer a solution when ordinary medicine has failed, or provide a gentle alternative. I would never recommend a herbal remedy instead of a visit to the doctor but it can sometimes be the answer to minor ailments, aches and pains.

Of course, most people are familiar with herbs and spices in the kitchen, and our food would be very dull and boring without them; even a very simple dish can be lifted into the realms of gourmet delight just by seasoning it with fresh herbs newly picked from the garden. I use the herb bed in our garden a great deal and would rather part with some more lawn than give up my herb supplies! I can thoroughly recommend a herb garden as an excellent use of space if you are wondering whether to experiment with growing your own herbs.

I hope you will enjoy this collection of herbal and spicy ideas and find that it encourages you to experiment with recipes, decorations and ideas that you might not have tried before.

JOANNA SHEEN

A LEXICON

OF

HERBS AND SPICES

*In this section you will find descriptions
of over forty of the herbs and spices that I
consider to be most useful, not only in the
kitchen but also for decorative purposes
and medicinal uses.*

Allium sativum
GARLIC

Garlic is one of the oldest known herbs and has been acknowledged as having powers of healing and, apparently, the ability to protect against evil spirits and vampires! It grows in bulbs which separate into individual cloves.

Cultivation tips
The plant is a hardy perennial and is grown by planting individual garlic cloves with the roots pointing downwards. Its smell deters many aphids so it is an excellent companion plant in fruit, vegetable and flower gardens.

Best way to preserve, dry or store
Garlic bulbs should be harvested about six months after the original cloves were planted, when the flowers are beginning to fade and the leaves are shrivelling. The traditional way to store garlic is in plaits (braids) formed by their leaves, and these plaits should be hung in a dry airy place. If the bulbs are kept in a moist atmosphere they will become mildewed and the smell can be quite overpowering.

Culinary and decorative uses
Garlic is one of the most popular additions to any cook's list of ingredients. It gives its own unique flavour to many dishes but the amount added to each recipe is a matter of personal taste. It goes well with many vegetables, most meats and sauces and can even be turned into garlic soup or pâté. Whole dried bulbs can be used for decorative purposes in wreaths and small dried arrangements.

Medicinal uses
Garlic essential oil is very rarely used on the skin because of its characteristically pungent smell. However, garlic capsules or pearls can be taken to combat infections, heart and circulatory problems and teenage acne, and to minimize hay fever and sinus attacks. Garlic is renowned for its ability to cleanse the blood.

History and myths
Garlic is thought to have originated in Siberia, but it is now grown in many areas of the world. It was much used by the Romans and Greeks, and in more modern times it was mentioned by both Chaucer and Shakespeare. Its medicinal properties have long been recognized – the Romans took garlic before marches to avoid infections and during the Middle Ages garlic was used to treat leprosy. Doctors used it during the Second World War as an effective antiseptic when treating wounds.

GARLIC

CHIVES

Allium schoenoprasum
CHIVES

These tufty plants resemble grass but their long round leaves have a delicate oniony smell and taste. They bear pinky-mauve pompom flowers.

Cultivation tips and varieties
Chives are hardy perennials that are easily grown from seed. Alternatively, the plants can be lifted and divided after flowering. *Allium schoenoprasum* are known as onion chives, but you can also grow garlic chives (*A. tuberosum*) which have white flowers. Their names indicate their flavours. Both varieties are excellent companion plants to vegetables, fruits and flowers susceptible to aphid attack.

Best way to preserve, dry or store
Chives should be used fresh whenever possible as they are not very appealing when dried. You can chop chives and freeze them with a little water in ice

cube trays, or make up chive butter and freeze that. The flowers can be air dried but they should be used in fairly generous bunches as they do not have a very striking appearance on their own.

Culinary and decorative uses
Fresh chives are a wonderful addition to many summer dishes and can also be used as a garnish. They should be added at the last minute to cooked dishes as overcooking ruins their flavour. Chive flowers can be included in a basket of mixed herbs or pressed for use in pictures.

Medicinal uses
Chives are thought to cleanse the blood, reduce blood pressure and act as a good general tonic.

History and myths
Chives have been grown for at least 5000 years, and probably originated in China. In his *Herbal*, Nicholas Culpeper wrote that he would have left chives out of his book if someone hadn't pointed out his omission; he went on to say they send 'very hurtful vapours to the brain'.

Anethum graveolens
DILL
Dill grows to about 1 metre (3 feet). It has fine feathery leaves and yellow umbels of flowers followed by flat seeds.

Cultivation tips
Dill is an annual which is sown in the spring or autumn, if the winters are fairly mild. Take care to keep it well away from fennel or the two will cross-pollinate and produce fill and dennel plants which don't have much flavour at all. Dill likes fertile, well-drained soil and is happiest in a sunny,

sheltered position. Water well during dry spells. Dill is a good companion plant to cabbages.

Best way to preserve, dry or store
The seeds are ready for harvesting after the plant has flowered. Cut the seed heads off the plant and place them on a baking sheet or wire cake rack and leave to dry in a warm airy place. When they are completely dry, shake out the seeds and store in a screw-top jar in a cool dark place. The leaves can be picked and dried before the flowers appear but they are better frozen – either by putting them with a little water in ice cube trays, or wrapping a bundle of leaves in foil before freezing. Both the flowers and leaves can be pressed and the flowers and seed heads picked on long stems and hung up in bunches for air drying.

Culinary and decorative uses
Dill is one of the most useful herbs for culinary purposes. The seed is excellent with vegetables and in pickles and chutneys. The flavour of the leaves (preferably fresh) is unsurpassed and is especially delicious in potato salads and with fish, egg and cheese dishes. The dried flowers and seed heads can be used in arrangements or pressed.

Medicinal uses
Dill essential oil is used in aromatherapy to treat colic, flatulence and indigestion. It can also promote the milk flow of nursing mothers. A few chopped leaves eaten every day in a salad are said to strengthen the hair and nails.

History and myths
Dill is a native of the Mediterranean but is cultivated throughout the world. The Egyptians used it as a

medicine and the Romans took it to Britain where, in the sixteenth and seventeenth centuries, it was believed to ward off evil spirits. The early settlers took some seeds with them to America.

Angelica archangelica
ANGELICA (GARDEN ANGELICA)
Angelica has serrated bright green leaves and thick, hollow stems that are not dissimilar to celery. One of the best-known uses for angelica stems is as a crystallized decoration.

Cultivation tips
Angelica is a biennial that reaches up to 2 metres (6 feet) high. It likes partial shade and a rich damp soil. It can be grown from seeds sown in late summer and transplanted the following spring. If some of the seeds are left on the plant it will usually seed itself, ready for the following year.

ANGELICA

Best way to preserve, dry or store
Harvest the seeds just before they fall by cutting off the whole flower heads and hanging them in bunches to air dry. Then shake out the seeds and store them in an airtight container in a dark place. The stems can be cut and used at any time of the year, but the leaves should be used when young. To harvest the roots, dig them up after the plant has set its seed, wash and store in an airy place until needed.

Culinary and decorative uses
The stems can be candied or crystallized and used to decorate sweets and cakes. Young leaves can be added to salads or fruit that is to be cooked. The seeds and roots give out a lovely perfume when burnt on a fire. Angelica leaves and flowers are pretty in posies of fresh herbs. In some parts of Scandinavia, the midribs of angelica leaves are steamed and eaten in the same way as asparagus.

Medicinal uses
In aromatherapy, angelica essential oil should never be used during pregnancy or by diabetics. At other times it is used to improve such skin conditions as psoriasis, treat anaemia, water retention, gout, fatigue and migraine. It is said that chewing angelica stems cures flatulence.

History and myths
Angelica is thought to have originated in northern Europe – probably Scandinavia and Russia. It was an ingredient in Carmelite water, a cordial made by Carmelite monks in Paris during the early seventeenth century. Angelica seeds were burnt in chafing dishes to fumigate and perfume houses, and the plant was thought to ward off witches and the Evil Eye and to protect against plague.

Anthemis nobilis
CAMOMILE

Camomile has small, daisy-like flowers and fine grey-green foliage. It has long been grown as a herb as well as for decorative, scented lawns.

Cultivation tips and varieties
There are several varieties of camomile but the three most popular varieties are Roman camomile (*Anthemis nobilis*) which is a perennial, German camomile (*Matricaria camomilla*) which is an annual and *A. n.* 'Treneague', which is a perennial and particularly suitable for lawns. All can be sown from seed. The flowers can be harvested from midsummer onwards, and the plants can be grown for edging and carpeting, so are extremely useful in the herb garden.

Best way to preserve, dry or store
To harvest the flowers, pick them with no stem and arrange on a flat sheet of paper or a baking sheet and leave in a warm room to dry naturally. When they are completely dry, store them in an airtight container in a warm dark place. The flowers can also be pressed, in which case they should be picked on the day they come into bloom.

Culinary and decorative uses
Fresh camomile flowers can be added to a salad. An infusion of camomile flowers can also be used in equal quantities with sparkling wine to make a light, refreshing summer drink. For decorative purposes, the flowers look very attractive in pressed flower pictures; they can also be used in pot pourris after being dried or pressed.

Medicinal uses
Several varieties of camomile are made into essential oil, and German

CAMOMILE

camomile is the most expensive. All are useful in aromatherapy, treating many skin complaints including acne, allergies, eczema, burns and rashes. Camomile oils can also combat menopausal and period problems, headaches, migraines and stress-related complaints. The main use of camomile flowers is in making soothing teas and tisanes to alleviate insomnia and indigestion. (Beatrix Potter's Peter Rabbit was given camomile tea to settle his stomach after he ate part of Mr McGregor's vegetable patch.)

History and myths
Camomile has been popular around the Mediterranean for more than 1500 years. The ancient Egyptians dedicated the herb to their gods, and it was also held sacred in Anglo-Saxon Europe.

Anthriscus cerefolium
CHERVIL

Chervil has a delicate, mildly aniseed, flavour that is much favoured in French cookery. The plant has bright green leaves, the flowers are small flat white umbels and the seeds look rather like caraway.

Cultivation tips
Chervil is a hardy annual that can be sown from seed in autumn or spring. It should be protected from frost and kept watered during long spells of drought. Cut it back several times during the season to stimulate fresh new growth. Chervil grows to about 45 cm (18 in) and will readily self-seed itself.

Best way to preserve, dry or store
Chervil flowers can be placed on a wire cake rack or baking sheet and left to dry naturally, then stored in an airtight container in a warm dark place. Fresh chervil leaves can be frozen in a little water in ice cube trays.

Culinary and decorative uses
Chervil is one of the four herbs used in French *fines herbes* – chives, parsley and tarragon are the others. When finely chopped it is excellent with eggs, vegetables and cheese. Chervil leaves and flowers can be pressed for use in pictures but are generally too delicate to be dried successfully.

Medicinal uses
Plenty of fresh chervil is said to be good for poor memory, depression, water retention and sluggish digestion. The essential oil is used extensively in the food industry but it is not used in aromatherapy.

CHERVIL

History and myths
Chervil has been grown for centuries, and is associated with Moses' blessing of the vessels of the Tabernacle. It is native to south-east Europe but, as the Romans took it to every country they invaded, it now grows all over the world. Early settlers in America took the seeds from British plants with them.

Armoracia rusticana
HORSERADISH

Horseradish has green leaves that look similar to spinach. The root system has a long tap root, with many smaller roots around it. It is this creamy white root that is used in cooking, medicine and for cosmetic purposes. It has a hot, peppery flavour.

Cultivation tips
Horseradish is a hardy perennial which likes rich moist soil and light shade. It grows to about 45-60 cm (18-24 in) and needs plenty of space in which to spread. It can be sown from seed, lifted and divided, or cuttings can be taken in the spring.

Best way to preserve, dry or store
The roots can be harvested at any time of year – dig up the plant, cut off the top growth and peel the roots before using. They can be stored in trays of damp sand until needed.

Culinary and decorative uses
Freshly grated horseradish is delicious in salads, butter and sauces. Horseradish sauce (grated horseradish, lemon and cream) is served with roast beef, but can be mixed with puréed apple and served with pork.

Medicinal uses
Grated horseradish can help to alleviate colds and bronchial complaints. When mixed with yoghurt it helps to fade freckles and relieve eczema. The essential oil is too toxic and irritant to be used at home.

History and myths
Horseradish is thought to have originated in eastern Europe but has spread to many countries since then. It is particularly popular in German, English and French cookery.

FRENCH
TARRAGON

Artemisia dracunculus
FRENCH TARRAGON

French tarragon has smooth narrow mid-green leaves and inconspicuous yellowy-green flowers.

Cultivation tips and varieties
French tarragon is a perennial that can be propagated from cuttings or division in the spring. It grows up to 60 cm (2 feet) tall and prefers a sheltered yet sunny position in rich, well-drained soil. Don't confuse it with Russian tarragon (*A. dracunculoides*), which has a very disappointing flavour.

Best way to preserve, dry or store
Pick individual leaves and arrange them on a wire cake rack to dry naturally. When they are completely dry they should be stored in an airtight container in a warm airy place.

Culinary and decorative uses
For culinary purposes, French tarragon is far superior to the Russian variety. It is especially useful in vinegars, and adds a delicious flavour to mayonnaise and sauces. Tarragon is an essential ingredient in the French *fines herbes* mixture added to egg dishes. It is excellent with chicken and other poultry, fish and shellfish and is used in such classic sauces as bearnaise and tartare. The decorative uses are very limited, but it can be an ingredient in fresh herb posies and wreaths.

Medicinal uses
Tarragon was once thought to have many medicinal uses, but it is now mainly considered to be good at curing digestive problems. The essential oil should not be used at home unless under the guidance of a professional aromatherapist, and never during pregnancy.

History and myths
Tarragon probably originated in central Asia and was taken to Europe by the Moors, but only became popular there from the seventeenth century onwards. In the past, it was believed that tarragon kept away venomous insects and snakes and could treat their bites.

Borago officinalis
BORAGE

Borage has rough hairy leaves and pretty deep blue star-shaped flowers that can be used to decorate summer drinks, salads and puddings.

Cultivation tips
Borage is a hardy annual that reaches about 60 cm (2 feet) in height. It does not transplant well and should therefore be sown from seed where it is to grow. Borage is happy in most situations although it prefers a sunny position in light soil. If you leave a few flowers on the plant it will self-seed itself, ensuring a flourishing crop for the following year.

Best way to preserve, dry or store
Borage leaves and flowers are best used fresh rather than dried. The flowers can be frozen by quarter-filling each unit of an ice cube tray with water and floating a borage flower in each one. Carefully fill up each unit with more water and freeze. These ice cubes can then be served in drinks at any time of year. The flowers can also be crystallized for use on cakes and puddings.

Culinary and decorative uses
Young borage leaves can be chopped and eaten in salads, or mixed with cream cheese in sandwiches. The leaves and flowers can be used in punches and wine cups. Decorative sprays of crystallized borage look wonderful on puddings and iced (frosted) cakes. The flowers can be pressed and used in herbal pictures but they are not suitable for drying.

BORAGE

Medicinal uses
Borage leaves, not the oil, are used in complementary medicine. The second half of borage's Latin name (*officinalis*) indicates that it was once used as a medicine. Compresses can be made from the leaves and wrapped around the legs to soothe painful or congested veins. Borage tea, made from fresh or dried flowers or leaves, is a good tonic for liver and kidney problems, and also eases the symptoms of feverish colds.

History and myths
Originally, borage was believed to impart courage to anyone who consumed it, so in medieval England borage tea was always drunk before jousting tournaments. It was also recommended as a cure for hypochondria and depression.

Calendula officinalis
MARIGOLD
Although usually thought of as a flower, this herb has many culinary and medicinal uses. The golden-orange petals give a lovely splash of colour in the garden, whether they are planted in the herb bed, herbaceous border or provide a summer display in pots and tubs.

Cultivation tips
The marigold is an annual that can be grown from seed with very little trouble and, once established, a clump of marigolds will steadily get larger and larger provided the winter weather is not so severe it kills them off. They can also still be in flower long after other plants have gone over and happily self-seed themselves from year to year. If they are cut back after their first flowering they will quickly be in bloom again.

Best way to preserve, dry or store
The flowers should be picked when they first start to bloom, then tied in small bunches and hung up to air dry.

Culinary and decorative uses
Fresh marigold petals look magnificent in summer salads and give a peppery flavour when mixed with cream cheese for a sandwich filling. Marigold flowers can also be added to rice dishes, and chopped finely to make marigold butter for garnishing meat and poultry. The dried flowers can be added to pot pourris and used on their stems or wired into dried flower arrangements.

MARIGOLD

Medicinal uses
The marigold was once considered to be an important medicinal plant, particularly for its ability to heal wounds, soothe inflamed eyes and stop bleeding, and it is still an ingredient in many homoeopathic preparations. Marigold tea, made from fresh petals, is said to soothe feverish colds. Calendula or marigold essential oil is excellent for treating skin complaints, including eczema, rashes, burns, bites

and stings. It can speed up the healing of wounds, cuts and abrasions. Commercially, the oil is one of the main ingredients in a cream that combats nappy (diaper) rash.

History and myths
The marigold originated in southern Europe and was taken to America by the early settlers. It has been given various meanings over the centuries – Chaucer linked it with jealousy, the Mexicans once believed it was the flower of death and it was originally associated with obedience.

Capsicum annuum
PAPRIKA
Paprika is one of the spices from the pepper family, but it is much sweeter and less fiery than chilli (chili pepper) – see *Capsicum frutescens*. The most famous centre for paprika is Hungary, where it is used in goulashes, amongst other dishes.

Cultivation
Paprika likes hot dry summers. The peppers are cone-shaped and a warm red colour.

Best way to preserve, dry or store
The peppers are harvested and dried at the end of the summer and then crushed. The powder is stored in an airtight container in a dark place.

Culinary and decorative uses
Although the most famous use for paprika is in goulash, it is also used in Spain and Portugal where it is added to fish dishes and sausages. It can also be used extensively in vegetarian cookery. For decorative purposes, the whole peppers can be used in the same way as chillies but they are not as easy to obtain.

Medicinal uses
There are few medicinal uses for paprika, but it does contain large amounts of vitamin C. The essential oil is not suitable for home use unless under professional guidance.

History and myths
Paprika originates from America, and was taken from there to Europe by Christopher Columbus.

Capsicum frutescens
CHILLI (CHILI PEPPER)
Chillies belong to the green and red pepper family but are not related to black and white peppercorns. Chillies are a rusty red colour and contain creamy white seeds, and their flavour can range from very mild to extremely hot. Take care not to rub your eyes, nose or mouth when handling fresh chillies as they can irritate your skin. Wear plastic or rubber gloves while preparing chillies. Removing the seeds before cooking helps to reduce the heat of the chillies.

Cultivation tips and varieties
The capsicum family contains many varieties of chilli, with varying degrees of heat. The colours include red, green, black and brown, and you might like to try the different varieties according to the recipe you are following. Although they are usually grown in very hot parts of the world they can be grown in greenhouses in more temperate climes.

Best way to preserve, dry or store
Chillies are available as a powder but you can also buy whole dried chillies and grind them as and when you want them – this enables you to cook with some and use others for decoration. Keep the chillies in an airtight

CHILLIES

container until needed. If you buy fresh chillies they should be kept in the refrigerator.

Culinary and decorative uses
The chilli pepper is used far and wide throughout many areas of the world. Chilli con carne is probably the best-known dish containing chillies, but they can also be used in curries, other Asian cooking and, of course, in Mexican recipes. The dried pods look wonderful as decorations when strung together, placed individually in arrangements and on floral plaques.

Medicinal uses
Chillies have few medical properties, but they do contain plenty of vitamin C. The essential oil is not suitable for home use unless under the guidance of a professional aromatherapist.

History and myths
Chillies have been used for flavouring in Peru and surrounding areas for thousands of years.

Carum carvi
CARAWAY
The small seeds of the caraway plant are used in the preparation of kummel in Germany and in cookery throughout central Europe. Caraway has a fairly strong and unique flavour.

Cultivation tips
The plant from which caraway seed comes is a biennial that grows to about 60 cm (2 feet) and produces pretty white flowers. It likes light well-drained soil and partial shade. Prune the plants well at the end of the first season and they will flower again the following summer.

Best way to preserve, dry or store
Leave the seeds to ripen on the plant, then cut them and hang them up in bunches. When the bunches have dried, the seeds can be shaken out and stored in an airtight jar.

Culinary and decorative uses
Caraway is delicious with cheese and bread and also in vegetable recipes – especially with root vegetables and cabbage. The seed is so tiny that I have found very few decorative uses for it, other than in collages.

Medicinal uses
In aromatherapy, caraway essential oil is used to treat flatulence, indigestion and poor appetite, as well as colds, coughs and laryngitis. Tea made from caraway seeds is said to have the same properties, and the seeds were originally put in cakes to make them more digestible.

History and myths
Caraway has been used as a spice for at least 4000 or 5000 years. It enjoyed a revival in Victorian Britain when it became a popular baking ingredient.

Cinnamomum zeylanicum
CINNAMON

Cinnamon is the bark taken from an Asiatic tree, *Cinnamomum zeylanicum*. It is a very useful spice for both culinary and decorative purposes and should be in everyone's store cupboard (pantry). It has a warm woody flavour.

Cultivation and varieties

The tree from which cinnamon is obtained, *Cinnamomum zeylanicum*, grows in China and Sri Lanka. The crop is harvested mainly by hand – the outer bark is removed and the inner bark peeled off and rolled into quills. Cassia, which is a closely related spice, comes from the *Cinnamomum cassia* tree and has a heavier, less delicate taste.

Best way to preserve, dry or store

Cinnamon is sold in sticks or powder, but if you buy the sticks you have the option of using them whole for decoration and grinding them down for recipes whenever you need them. I find this works better than buying the ready powdered variety as it seems to lose its fragrance very quickly.

Culinary and decorative uses

There are many culinary uses for cinnamon, but I confess that my favourite is in cappuccino coffee – you can either sprinkle the powder on top or stir the coffee with a cinnamon stick. Apple and cinnamon are a magical combination, and the spice is also used in mulled wine and in baking generally. The whole sticks (which can be bought in a variety of sizes) are indispensable for decorations and look wonderful when arranged in bundles on wreaths, Christmas trees or on the top of pot pourris. The best sticks to use for decorative purposes are the cassia sticks as they are longer and heavier than ordinary ones.

Medicinal uses

If using cinnamon essential oil at home, make sure it is distilled from the leaves and not the bark – cinnamon bark oil is very hazardous and should only be used by professional aromatherapists. Cinnamon leaf essential oil can be used as a mild antiseptic, to stimulate the circulation and breathing, and to ease digestive problems. It blends well with orange and clove essential oils for Christmas pot pourris. Tea made from cinnamon is said to calm nausea.

History and myths

Cinnamon is one of the oldest plants known to man and is mentioned in Exodus in the Bible. The Chinese have been using it for over 2000 years for both culinary and medicinal purposes. There are also stories about the strong aphrodisiac powers of cinnamon.

Coriandrum sativum
CORIANDER

Both the small yellow seeds of coriander and the bright green leaves are popular in cookery as a spice and herb respectively. The leaves are also known as cilantro or Chinese parsley. The plant is grown in many areas of the world and has a deliciously fresh, yet spicy taste.

Cultivation tips

Coriander is an annual which grows to about 45 cm (18 in) and resembles parsley, to which it is loosely related. It grows well in southern Europe and America and also in the Middle East, so likes a sunny position and light, dry soil. Sow the seed in the place where you want the plants to grow.

Best way to preserve, dry or store

Coriander leaves (cilantro) are used fresh and can be gathered whenever they are required. Only pick as many as you will need because they wilt and do not keep well. Leave the seeds on the plant until they have become completely ripe and are a grey colour. Cut off the seed heads and leave them to dry for a couple of days, then shake out the seeds and store in an airtight jar in a dark but warm place.

Culinary and decorative uses

The Chinese use a tremendous amount of coriander (particularly the leaves) in their cooking, and the seeds are used widely in Greek, Mexican and Indian cookery. The seeds can be used to flavour bread, curries, pickles and

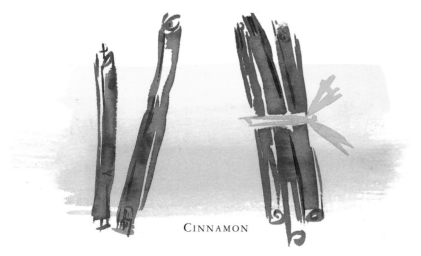

CINNAMON

CORIANDER

sauces. The leaves can be chopped into soups, sauces and curries, and used as a garnish. Decoratively, the seeds are too small for most craft work.

Medicinal uses
A tea made from coriander seeds is a common remedy for indigestion. Coriander essential oil can be used to treat poor circulation, rheumatism, digestive problems, colds, flu and nervous exhaustion.

History and myths
The coriander plant has long associations with love potions and aphrodisiac medicines. Some Arabian tribes use coriander to ease labour pains and to regulate the reproductive system. Coriander is one of the flavourings in liqueurs such as Benedictine and Chartreuse.

Crocus sativus
SAFFRON
The feathery yellow strands of saffron are actually the dried stigmas of the autumn-flowering saffron crocus. The stigmas have to be separated from the mauve-purple petals, and it takes about 70 000 flowers to yield 450 g (1 lb) of saffron, which is why saffron is the most expensive spice in the world.

Cultivation tips
The saffron crocus, *Crocus sativus*, grows best in Mediterranean countries, and particularly on the plains of La Mancha in Spain, so try to reproduce these dry, warm conditions when growing the plant yourself. The corms are planted in July and the flowers harvested in September, when the stigmas can be dried and preserved.

Best way to preserve, dry or store
The flower blooms in the autumn for a few weeks, and the harvesting is traditionally done by hand. These precious strands should be stored in an airtight container in a dark place at room temperature.

Culinary and decorative uses
Spanish paella is one of the best-known dishes incorporating saffron, but it is also used in Italian, French and Middle Eastern, as well as Jewish, recipes. Saffron is only used for decorative purposes in dyeing and colouring food and clothing.

Medicinal uses
Throughout the centuries, saffron was considered excellent for relieving nervous troubles.

History and myths
Saffron is mentioned in the Song of Solomon in the Bible, and its use is widespread throughout the Greek, Roman and Arab cultures. It was once prized for its medicinal properties as well as its colour.

SAFFRON

Cuminum cyminum
CUMIN

Cumin seeds look similar to caraway and aniseed but they smell quite different. They are most popularly used in tandoori dishes in Indian cookery. It is also rumoured that feeding the seeds to pigeons helps to keep them healthy!

Cultivation tips
Cumin is a half-hardy annual that grows about 15 cm (6 in) high and bears tiny white or mauve flowers. The seeds are only produced during very hot summers.

Best way to preserve, dry or store
Cut the stems of the plants before the seeds are fully ripe and hang them up to air dry in a warm place – the seeds only develop their true flavour when completely dry. Store in an airtight container in a dark airy place.

Culinary and decorative uses
Cumin seeds can be ground or used whole, and add a unique flavour to meat, fish and poultry dishes. There are also many vegetable recipes that include cumin. The seeds are too small to have many decorative uses.

Medicinal uses
Avoid using the essential oil during pregnancy as it can produce adverse effects. At other times, cumin oil can treat poor circulation, flatulence and migraine. It is often used in veterinary medicines to aid digestion.

History and myths
Although cumin originated in the East, it has been grown in the Mediterranean for over 1000 years. Cumin is mentioned in both the Old and New Testaments and was very popular during the Middle Ages.

Curcuma longa
TURMERIC

Turmeric is a rhizome, or underground root, and is related to ginger (see *Zingiber officinale*). It is most widely used in Indian cuisine to give a strong golden colour and its own aromatic flavour.

Cultivation
The plant has large leaves. It is now grown in several countries, including China, India and Jamaica. The knobbly roots are boiled and then peeled to reveal the yellow interior. They are then dried and ground.

Best way to preserve, dry or store
It is rare to see turmeric in any other form than powdered. Buy it in small quantities from a shop with a regular turnover to ensure it is fresh, and store in an airtight container.

Culinary and decorative uses
Turmeric is mainly used in curries, and is especially delicious in smoked fish curries. Decoratively, the yellow colour is used as a form of dye in Asian cosmetics but it has little other value.

Medicinal uses
Turmeric essential oil is used in aromatherapy to treat arthritis, rheumatism, anorexia and liver congestion. However, you should use it in moderation because it can be slightly toxic or act as an irritant. During the Middle Ages in Europe, doctors thought it cured jaundice.

History and myths
Turmeric has been grown in India for many thousands of years and was used as a spice in biblical times. It is used to colour festive dishes in the Middle East. Hindus associate turmeric with fertility.

Elettaria cardamomum
CARDAMOM

The pods containing the cardamom seeds are about 0.12-2.5 cm ($^1/_2$-1 in) long and have a fragrant scent. They can be used whole or the seeds removed and crushed before use.

Cultivation
Cardamom pods come from *Elettaria cardamomum* – a plant related to the ginger family which grows in tropical rain forests. It is therefore difficult to cultivate in any other climate.

Best way to preserve, dry or store
The pale green pods are harvested just before they are completely ripe, then dried slowly to preserve their essential oils. The pods should be kept in an airtight container in a dark place once they are dry.

Culinary and decorative uses
Cardamom is probably most familiar as the spice sprinkled over coffee in the Middle East, but it is also used extensively in curries, rice dishes and with pulses. The attractively coloured pods can be used to fill small gaps between other spices or flowers when making pomanders.

Medicinal uses
A tea made from crushed cardamom seeds is believed to aid digestion, soothe morning sickness and, when used as a gargle, can soothe sore throats. In aromatherapy, the essential oil is used to treat digestive disorders, such as vomiting, heartburn, colic and stomach cramps. It can also ease mental fatigue and nervous strain.

History and myths
Although cardamom has been popular in many countries for some time, there are no special stories associated with it.

Eugenia aromatica
CLOVES

Cloves are small dried flower buds, and have such a strong smell and flavour that people love or hate them.

Cultivation tips

Cloves are harvested from the evergreen tree, *Eugenia aromatica*, which grows up to 12 metres (36 feet) tall and has bright green leaves. The clove tree is also called *E. caryophyllus*.

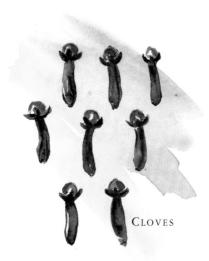

CLOVES

Best way to preserve, dry or store

Whole cloves are often used in cookery, although powdered cloves are also useful. It is easiest to grind a few whole cloves when you need them rather than stock both the whole and powdered versions. Cloves should be stored in small airtight jars.

Culinary and decorative uses

Cloves are used to spice mulled wines and ales, to stud the skins of hams and in curries. They are also useful in puddings and cakes. Decoratively, cloves are best known as ingredients in pomanders – whole cloves are stuck into oranges or apples which are then rolled in powdered orris root and displayed in rooms where their delicious spicy smell will be enjoyed.

Medicinal uses

Oil of cloves has been used as an antiseptic and mild anaesthetic for centuries. When buying it for home use, ensure the oil has been extracted from clove buds and not the leaves or stems. Oil of cloves is often used to relieve pain in the mouth and also to treat infections and nervous tension.

History and myths

Cloves have always been grown in several different parts of the world, but the finest ones are reputed to come from the island of Grenada. The Indonesians smoke rolled cloves and they were ingredients in aphrodisiac potions in ancient Persia.

Foeniculum vulgare
FENNEL

The green or bronze feathery leaves of fennel are beautiful, so it can look lovely in the herb garden or herbaceous border. Both the leaves and the seeds have an aniseed-like flavour.

Cultivation tips

Fennel is a herbaceous perennial that reaches about 1.6-2 metres (5-6 feet) very quickly, so plant it at the back of the border. You can either cut back the foliage hard each autumn to encourage new growth the following spring, or harvest the whole plant (the bulb is a delicious vegetable) and sow some of its seeds the following spring for a new crop of plants.

Best way to preserve, dry or store

The leaves do not dry well at all, but they can be frozen – either wrap a bundle of them in foil or place small amounts in a little water in ice cube trays. However, the seeds can be dried by cutting off the seed heads and leaving them in a warm airy place. When they are completely dry, shake out the seeds and store them in a screw-top jar. Fennel flowers can be dried if they are cut just after their yellow colour is at its strongest but before they go over.

Culinary and decorative uses

Fennel has similar uses to dill in cookery, but it is especially good with fish and the bulb makes a really delicious vegetable when steamed and then served with butter and black pepper. The yellow flowers are not very striking when dried but they are useful shapes for dried flower arrangements. Both the leaves and the flowers can be pressed.

Medicinal uses

Fennel oil has long been an ingredient in commercial cough mixtures, gripe water for babies and laxatives. If using it at home, always choose the sweet,

FENNEL

not bitter, fennel essential oil. It should be used in moderation and avoided completely during pregnancy. Sweet fennel oil is used in aromatherapy for skin care, the treatment of bruises, asthma, bronchitis, constipation, nausea and problems during the menopause.

History and myths
Greek athletes ate fennel to give them longevity, courage and strength. It is a native of the Mediterranean and was introduced to northern Europe by the Romans; in Britain it was one of the nine sacred herbs of the Anglo-Saxons. The Spanish introduced fennel to America and the Shakers later grew it commercially. Fennel has always been popular as a strewing herb and is used to keep away fleas when mixed with straw in kennels and stables.

Juniperus species
JUNIPER
Juniper is under-rated as a spice but is well worth seeking out as it can add a very special flavour to a dish. The best-known use for juniper berries is in the manufacture of gin. The berries are a deep purple-black and do not shrivel up when they have been dried.

Cultivation tips
The juniper is an evergreen tree that is often grown as a shrub. It is native to Europe, North America, Asia and North Africa, and will grow well in any soil.

Best way to preserve, dry or store
Unripe berries are green and should not be harvested until they have ripened and turned dark purple. They should be dried on flat baking sheets in a warm room and stored in an airtight container.

JUNIPER

Culinary and decorative uses
Juniper is the perfect addition to game dishes or strong beef recipes, but it is also successful with cabbage or potatoes. The berries can only be used in small-scale decorative items but they look attractive and are fun to use.

Medicinal uses
Juniper berries were burnt during the Middle Ages to ward off the plague, and the essential oil has long been acknowledged for its antiseptic powers. However, it should never be used during pregnancy. It is a good tonic for nerves, aids digestion, reduces water retention and soothes muscular aches and pains. Veterinary preparations for combating ticks and fleas include juniper oil.

History and myths
Juniper berries were used in Elizabethan times to make aqua vitae, and they are ingredients for drinks and tonics in several countries.

Laurus nobilis
BAY
The bay is a very large and attractive evergreen tree with fairly narrow glossy leaves. Shaped bay trees grown in tubs are very popular when placed on either side of a doorway or path.

Cultivation tips
Bay is an evergreen tree that likes a rich soil and a sheltered spot – its leaves can be burnt by cold winds and hard frosts. Tubs should be sheltered or brought indoors during the winter. Bay is propagated from cuttings taken in midsummer.

Best way to preserve, dry or store
The leaves can be used fresh, all year round. To dry the leaves, remove them from the tree, place on a wire cake rack and leave to dry naturally, then store in an airtight container. To use bay decoratively, you may wish to cut longer branches and hang them up to air dry.

Culinary and decorative uses
Bay leaves are best known as an ingredient in bouquet garni – a bundle of herbs used to flavour soups, stews and sauces. Bay can also be used in milk puddings to give a subtle flavour and is excellent in potted meats and pâtés. Dried sprays and branches of bay leaves are very useful in herb and dried flower arrangements and a topiary tree made from dried bay leaves can look very effective. Fresh bay leaves look magnificent in wreaths or as edgings to baskets and plates.

Medicinal uses
The bay tree has been considered an important medicinal plant for many centuries, especially as a protection against plague. A bath containing an infusion of bay leaves is good for

relieving aching limbs. In aromatherapy, bay essential oil can treat colds, tonsillitis, sprains and bruises, viral infections, dyspepsia, flatulence and loss of appetite, but it should never be used during pregnancy, always in moderation and preferably under the guidance of a professional aromatherapist. Bay oil can also be an ingredient of insect repellents.

BAY

History and myths

The Romans and Greeks believed bay was a sacred tree, so fashioned its leaves into wreaths and garlands to celebrate their victories. They also crowned their greatest poets with these garlands, hence the accolade 'poet laureate'. Bay was said to protect against lightning, witches and evil.

Lavandula species
LAVENDER

Lavender has soft grey-green foliage with very narrow needle-like leaves and flowers in various shades of pink, white and mauve. It is one of my favourite plants in the garden and is one I would never be without.

Cultivation tips and varieties

There are many varieties of lavender, but one of the most common is *Lavandula angustifolia*, a shrub that grows to about 60-100 cm (2-3 feet). More unusual varieties include French lavender (*Lavandula stoechas*), which has round flower heads topped with coloured bracts and a strong balsamic smell, and white lavender (*L. a.* 'Nana Alba'). All varieties need a sunny dry position and will not thrive in damp conditions. The easiest way to cultivate lavender is to take cuttings in late spring.

Best way to preserve, dry or store

To preserve the greatest amount of oil in the plants, and therefore ensure the greatest scent, pick and dry lavender before the last flowers on each stalk (stem) have opened. Gather into small bunches and hang up in a warm airy place to dry thoroughly.

Culinary and decorative uses

Although there are limited culinary uses for lavender there are a few recipes that work extremely well, such as lavender mustard and lavender biscuits (cookies). It is also delicious mixed with the syrup of a fresh fruit salad. Decoratively, lavender is invaluable and looks marvellous whether arranged on its own or with other herbs and flowers. When stripped from their stems, the flowers can be used to perfume sachets and pot pourris. Bundles of the stalks can be burnt on a

LAVENDER

log fire to fill the room with an aromatic scent.

Medicinal uses

Lavender has been used medicinally, mostly for its powerful antiseptic properties, since at least the first century AD, and was one of the herbs used for strewing floors in the Middle Ages. Lavender essential oil is one of the most valuable and versatile aromatherapy oils, and is a must for every medicine cabinet. It treats many skin conditions including acne, allergies, bruises, burns, sunburn, wounds, insect bites and stings, and acts as an insect repellent. It can also treat throat infections, asthma, nausea, flu, nasal congestion and is especially good for migraine, headaches, nervous tension and other stress-related conditions. It is one of the very few essential oils that can be used neat on the skin (but try a patch test first).

History and myths
Lavender was known to the Greeks and is mentioned in the Bible as 'spikenard'. The Romans used it in washing water for linen (the name lavender comes from *lavare*, the Latin for 'to wash'), then brought it to Britain, where it has always been one of the most popular perfumes.

Levisticum officinale
LOVAGE

Lovage looks a little like a smaller version of angelica crossed with celery. It has yellow flowers followed by brown seeds, and tastes like a slightly stronger and more peppery version of celery.

Cultivation tips
Lovage is a hardy herbaceous perennial that gets bigger every year until it eventually reaches up to 2 metres (6 feet) or more. It likes a shady position, rich soil and plenty of water.

Best way to preserve, dry or store
The flower heads can be harvested before the seeds start to fall, tied into small bunches and hung up to air dry. The seeds can be harvested by cutting off the seed heads, leaving them to dry completely, then shaking out the seeds and storing them in screw-top jars in a warm airy place. Sprays of leaves can be wrapped in foil and stored in the freezer until needed.

Culinary and decorative uses
The stalks (stems) of lovage are sometimes crystallized in the same way as angelica. The leaves are an excellent addition to salads and make good garnishes. The flower heads can be dried for use in herbal arrangements. The seeds can be added to bread, cakes and biscuits (cookies).

Medicinal uses
An infusion of lovage leaves is said to soothe sore throats and can be dabbed on wounds to speed the healing process. Lovage essential oil should not be used during pregnancy, but at other times it is useful in the treatment of digestive disorders, flatulence, poor circulation, water retention and cystitis.

History and myths
Lovage originates from around the Mediterranean and was a widely used herb from Roman times, especially by Benedictine monks in the treatment of fevers. Lovage stems were often eaten as a vegetable and the whole plant was considered to be an aphrodisiac and a lucky charm in love. Its popularity waned from the nineteenth century onwards, and it is not as widely used today as it should be.

LOVAGE

Melissa officinalis
LEMON BALM (BALM)

This is a sweet-scented herb with bright green leaves and small white flowers. When bruised, the leaves give off a delicious lemony scent. They also taste of lemon.

Cultivation tips
Lemon balm is a hardy herbaceous perennial that likes a partly sunny position with plenty of moisture. It can be grown from seed, propagated from cuttings in the spring or lifted and divided in the autumn. Cut the plants back hard each autumn to encourage fresh growth the following spring.

Best way to preserve, dry or store
To dry the foliage, cut off long stems just as the plant is coming into flower, tie them into small bunches and hang them up to air dry. When completely dry, store the leaves in screw-top jars in a warm airy place.

Culinary and decorative uses
The delicate lemon flavour of the leaves blends well with chicken, duck and game. Lemon balm can also be used with many fish and in stuffings. Fresh leaves are delicious in green salads, fruit salads, summer punches and fruit cups.

Medicinal uses
An infusion of lemon balm is good for soothing feverish colds, and it can also help insomnia and various nervous complaints. In aromatherapy, melissa is a popular essential oil that is used extensively to alleviate anxiety, depression, high blood pressure, insomnia and migraine. It can also help with eczema and other skin problems, asthma and digestive disorders.

LEMON BALM

History and myths

Lemon balm was first found in the mountains of southern Europe, but it now grows naturally in many northern countries. It was considered sacred in the Temple of Diana and has always been associated with bees and their honey as it is very attractive to bees.

Mentha species
MINT

Mint is one of the best-known and widely used herbs, with a characteristically refreshing and cooling flavour.

Cultivation tips and varieties

There are many different varieties of mint, although spearmint (*Mentha spicata*), peppermint (*M. x piperita*) and apple mint (*M. suaveolens* syn. *M. rotundifolia*) are the most useful in the kitchen. Other interesting mints include pineapple, ginger, black and lemon. Root division is the easiest way to increase stocks of mint, but most varieties can also be grown from seed. However, normally the problem is keeping mint in check, because it is very invasive. The best way to do this is to plant it in a plastic bucket and then bury the bucket in the soil until only its rim is visible. All mints need full sun but plenty of water, and should be cut back after flowering.

Best way to preserve, dry or store

All mints can be picked with or without their flowers and hung up in bunches to air dry, after which they should be stored in airtight containers in a warm airy place. Alternatively, small sprigs of mint can be frozen with a little water in ice cube trays and dropped into drinks, or into dishes while they are being cooked.

Culinary and decorative uses

There are many ways to use mint in the kitchen, especially in Middle Eastern cookery, and one of the best-known British uses must be as mint sauce or jelly with lamb. A sprig of fresh mint is delicious with new potatoes or peas, but the more adventurous cook will also use this herb in puddings and soups. Many summer drinks, such as Pimms and mint juleps, would not be the same without it. Mint is an ingredient in the production of *crème de menthe*, Chartreuse and Benedictine. For decorative purposes, the mint foliage and flowers can be quite useful but they are rather brittle when dried and must be handled with care. Loose dried leaves and flowers can be incorporated into pot pourris.

Medicinal uses

Tea made from fresh or dried mint leaves is very refreshing and excellent for digestive disorders and feverish colds. In aromatherapy, peppermint essential oil has several uses, particularly in treating respiratory infections, muscle fatigue, mental exhaustion, stress and digestive disorders. Adding a few drops of the oil to a bowl of boiling water and inhaling the steam will help to soothe catarrh, sinusitis, asthma and bronchitis.

History and myths

The Greeks and Romans used mint to scent their bath water and to decorate tables at feasts. Mint was also used by monks in Saxon Britain to such an extent that it became known as the monks' herb. Its fresh scent made it an ideal strewing herb, and it was believed to stop milk turning sour.

MINT

Monarda didyma
BERGAMOT (OSWEGO TEA)
Bergamot has shaggy flower heads in pink, purple, red or white. They are rich in nectar and therefore very attractive to bees.

Cultivation tips
Bergamot is a perennial that grows to about 60-100 cm (2-3 feet), so it is best placed at the back of the herb bed. It is happy in either full sun or partial shade but needs a rich moist soil. Lift and divide the plants every few years and trim them back hard each autumn to encourage new growth in the spring.

Best way to preserve, dry or store
Bergamot leaves and flowers can be gathered in late summer, when the plant is in full bloom, and hung in small bunches to air dry. Alternatively, individual sprigs may be laid out on a wire cake rack and left to dry. The dried herbs should be stored in an airtight container in a warm dry place.

Culinary and decorative uses
Bergamot is a native of America and Canada and was cultivated in many early American gardens and used to make tea. The most famous tea made from the herb is Earl Grey, which originally combined bergamot with Indian tea leaves (today the tea is made from oil of bergamot). Dried leaves can be used as an alternative to mint, and fresh ones can be torn and added to a salad or chopped up in herb butters and soft cheese mixtures. Dried flower heads are a lovely addition to pot pourris and they can also be used for some decorative arrangements, although they are very delicate.

BERGAMOT

Medicinal uses
The fresh or dried leaves of bergamot can be added to a hot bath to revive aching limbs. Oil of bergamot is distilled from a small citrus tree, *Citrus bergamia*, and not this herb; it is used to treat digestive disorders, fevers and combat fatigue. Wait at least four hours after using the oil before going out in the sun or it may stain the skin.

History and myths
The herb is native to North America and was used by the American Indians to make tea. In the eighteenth century, bergamot was brought to Europe where it was also popular for tea-making.

Myristica fragrans
MACE AND NUTMEG
Mace and nutmeg come from the same plant, *Myristica fragrans*. The nutmeg is the central nut and is covered with a shiny dark brown shell; this in turn has a red lacy coating (the mace) which, when dried in the sun, becomes a pretty rusty apricot colour.

Cultivation
Mace and nutmeg grow on an evergreen tree with leaves that look rather similar to bay leaves. It grows in tropical climates, such as Grenada and Indonesia.

Best way to preserve, dry or store
Nutmeg can be bought surrounded by mace but the most usual way is to buy the two spices separately. They should be bought whole, not powdered, and ground or grated as and when required for maximum flavour.

Culinary and decorative uses
Nutmeg can be used in puddings (especially rice pudding), cakes and biscuits (cookies), but is also excellent with vegetables, notably cabbage and spinach. It is also added to mulled wine. Mace is excellent with potted meats and fish, especially prawns and shrimps, and is also good in sweet dishes. Decorative uses abound for individual nutmegs but they are quite expensive when used in bulk. Blades of mace give a dainty touch to spicy posies and decorations.

Medicinal uses

Nutmeg was once regarded as an important medicinal spice, especially in combating plague. The essential oil should be used with care during pregnancy, but its aromatherapy uses include the treatment of frigidity and impotence, bacterial infections, gout and sluggish digestion.

MACE AND
NUTMEG

History and myths

Nutmeg was mentioned by Shakespeare and Chaucer and has long been a great mainstay in kitchens and medicine cupboards. The perfume was greatly admired.

Ocimum basilicum
BASIL

There are several varieties of basil that can be grown, but they are all natives of the Far East and so flourish best on sunny windowsills or in greenhouses when grown in more temperate climates. The glossy deep green leaves are excellent with many dishes but are particularly popular in Mediterranean cookery. Basil has a warm and spicy flavour.

Cultivation tips and varieties

There are over 150 varieties of basil, but the ones most commonly grown are sweet basil (*Ocimum basilicum*) and bush basil (*O. b. minimum*). Lettuce-leaf basil and purple basil (*O. b. purpurascens*) are also popular. The herb is a tender annual and must have sunny yet moist conditions if it is to thrive. It grows best in pots and is an excellent companion plant to tomatoes. It is susceptible to the slightest frost.

Best way to preserve, dry or store

The leaves can be cut fresh from the plant whenever they are needed. To dry, harvest the long leafy stalks (stems) just before the plant comes into flower and dry them slowly on a wire cake rack or in tiny bunches. When they are completely dry, store in airtight containers in a dark place at room temperature.

Culinary and decorative uses

Basil is used in a great number of Italian dishes, particularly with tomatoes and other vegetables. One of the best known uses for basil is when it is mixed with pine nuts, olive oil and Parmesan cheese to produce pesto sauce, which is sublime with pasta. Dried basil is not very decorative but could be included in a basket of mixed dried herbs and foliage.

Medicinal uses

Fresh basil has long been regarded as an important health-giving herb, and some herbalists believed it induced cheerfulness (perhaps because it tastes so good). In aromatherapy, basil essential oil should not be used during pregnancy. At other times, it is used in skin care, to ward off insects and soothe insect bites. It is also a nerve tonic (although too much of it can cause depression), helpful in combating stress, beneficial to the respiratory, digestive and immune systems and can cure warts.

History and myths

Basil has been grown for at least 4000 years, and is regarded as sacred to Hindus in India, where it is used to protect against evil. It has long been associated with mythical serpents and was therefore used to draw out the poison from insect stings and bites. The Egyptian, Greek and Roman cultures all have many legends concerning basil.

BASIL

Origanum species
MARJORAM AND OREGANO
Both these herbs belong to the
Origanum family and have very similar
uses and tastes. However, they are
quite different when used decoratively.
Marjoram has deep purple flowers and
long stems, while oregano has small
light green flowers on short stems.

Cultivation tips and varieties
Several varieties of marjoram can be
grown, including sweet or knotted
marjoram (*Origanum majorana*), which
should be treated as an annual;
oregano (*O. vulgare*), which is a hardy
perennial; and pot or French marjoram
(*O. onites*), which is a herbaceous
perennial with a stronger flavour than
oregano. All these plants are easily
sown from seed or propagated from
cuttings in the spring. The plants
often become woody and are best
replaced every three or four years.
They all love sunny and dry
conditions.

Best way to preserve, dry or store
Both herbs can be picked just as they
are coming into full flower and hung
in small bunches in a warm airy place
until they are completely dry. If you
want to use them for culinary purposes
they should then be stored in airtight
containers in a warm airy place.

Culinary and decorative uses
Marjoram is one of the herbs used in
bouquet garni, together with parsley,
thyme and bay. It is a subtle, sweet-
flavoured herb that goes well with
sausages, stuffings and stews, and is
also excellent with vegetable dishes
containing tomatoes, beans and nuts.
Oregano is slightly stronger and is
good with rice, pasta dishes and pizzas.
Decoratively, both herbs are invaluable
for their form and colour.

MARJORAM AND OREGANO

Medicinal uses
Marjoram and oregano have been used
as medicinal herbs since the time of
the ancient Greeks, who used them as
antidotes to poisoning. A tea made
from the herbs is good for the
digestion and an excellent
tranquillizer. For aromatherapy,
choose sweet marjoram essential oil,
which is distilled from *Origanum
majorana*. It should not be used during
pregnancy and should always be used
in moderation. It can treat chilblains,
bruises, digestive problems, muscular
aches and pains, colds, headaches and
nervous tension. Marjoram essential
oil, distilled from *Origanum vulgare*,
should not be used at home unless
under the guidance of a professional
aromatherapist, and never during
pregnancy.

History and myths
Marjoram and oregano both originate
from the Mediterranean area but they
are now widely grown in many parts of
the world. In Roman times, wreaths
made from marjoram were worn by the
bride and groom at weddings, and the
Greeks believed that planting
marjoram on graves helped the dead to
sleep peacefully. Marjoram was a
strewing herb to sweeten the air of
public places and was popular in
Tudor and Stuart England as a plant
grown in knot gardens.

Papaver somniferum
POPPY SEED

The poppy seeds that we use in the kitchen actually come from the same plant as opium but have none of the drug's properties. The tiny blue-black seeds are either used whole or ground and have a slightly bitter taste.

Cultivation tips and varieties
Poppy seeds come from *Papaver somniferum*, the opium poppy, which can be easily grown from seed in the garden. There are several other varieties of poppy which can also be grown for decorative use, and they often self-seed themselves around the garden.

Best way to preserve, dry or store
As soon as the seed heads are ripe, they can be cut and air dried (don't hang them upside down or all the seeds will fall out of the pods). When the seed heads are completely dry, cut them in half and shake out the seeds. Store in an airtight container in a dry, dark place.

Culinary and decorative uses
Many European breads and pastries are sprinkled with whole poppy seeds, but they can also be ground to season and thicken curries. Whole poppy seed heads are extremely useful and attractive for decorative work and, if necessary, you could first extract the seeds by either shaking them out of the top or making a tiny hole in the seed pod. They can be used in their natural state or gilded for Christmas arrangements. Poppy seeds themselves are too small to be used in most decorations.

Medicinal uses
Poppies were once valued as medicines for their narcotic and sleep-inducing properties, but they are definitely not recommended for home use!

History and myths
The Romans, Egyptians and Greeks all loved poppy seeds, which were believed to give extra energy to the Olympic athletes in Greece.

Petroselinum crispum
PARSLEY

The bright green curled leaves of parsley are easy to identify and add a lovely splash of colour when used as a garnish. It has a fresh, slightly spicy and peppery taste.

Cultivation tips and varieties
Curled parsley, or *Petroselinum sativum*, is harder to grown than *P. crispum*, or Italian parsley. Both can be grown from seed in the spring, but the soil must be kept moist while the seed germinates. Although parsley is a biennial it is better to sow fresh stocks every year to ensure good plants.

Best way to preserve, dry or store
Parsley can be hung up in small bunches and left to air dry, or frozen in a little water in ice cube trays. However, parsley is really best eaten freshly picked from the plant. Parsley butter can be frozen and is a useful garnish for steaks, chops and potatoes.

Culinary and decorative uses
Parsley is one of the four herbs used in bouquet garni and is very useful in the kitchen. Parsley sauce is delicious with fish but also with cheese, egg and vegetable dishes. Chopped parsley is good in salads and gives a lift to sandwich fillings. The herb is difficult to use decoratively because dried parsley is very brittle, but it looks pretty in fresh herb bouquets, wreaths and posies.

Medical uses
Chewing a sprig of fresh parsley after eating garlic is said to sweeten the breath. Parsley is rich in many important trace elements, as well as vitamins A, B and C. The essential oil should be avoided during pregnancy but it can be used in moderation at other times to treat rheumatism, sciatica and arthritis, and to alleviate urinary infections and cystitis.

History and myths
Parsley was cultivated by the Greeks, who used it as a sacred herb in their burial rituals, and the Romans, and it was one of the plants grown in the garden of the Emperor Charlemagne. It is not always easy to grow and an old wives' tale says that it only thrives in gardens when the wife wears the trousers. (I'm not saying whether our parsley grows well or not...)

Pimenta officinalis
ALLSPICE

This small berry, which resembles a black peppercorn, is very versatile and can be used in both sweet and savoury dishes. It tastes like a combination of cinnamon, nutmeg and clove.

Cultivation

Allspice is grown mainly in Jamaica on large evergreen trees that reach up to 10 metres (30 feet) tall. *Pimenta officinalis* is slow to bear fruit but, once mature, the tree will produce allspice berries for many years – in some cases, up to 90 years or more.

Best way to preserve, dry or store

This is not something to grow yourself – just buy the berries and store them in an airtight tin or container. Allspice is also sold in powdered form, but it is best to buy the whole berries and grind them in a peppermill or coffee grinder as and when you want the powder.

Culinary and decorative uses

Allspice is used to spice pickle mixtures for herrings and beef, but it can also be used with fruit and puddings. For decorations, the berries can be soaked in water and then strung on to threads or used individually in small-scale work.

Medicinal uses

The essential oil can be extracted from both the leaves and berries of the allspice tree. The oil can be used in aromatherapy to alleviate rheumatism, general stiffness and arthritis; to ease coughs and bronchitis; to soothe indigestion and nausea; and to treat depression, tension and stress to the nervous system. Only use small amounts of the oil to avoid irritating the skin. Allspice oil is also used extensively in spicy and oriental perfumes.

History and myths

Allspice has only been used in Europe for about 400 years – considerably less than spices like caraway and cumin. It was sometimes confused with peppers as it looked similar.

Pimpinella anisum
ANISEED

Aniseed is a well-known flavouring, and is used in such alcoholic drinks as ouzo and Pernod. Aniseed sweets (candies) are childhood favourites and the spice is said to help digestion. Aniseed should not be confused with star anise, which has a similar flavour but comes from a different plant and is used mainly in Chinese cookery.

Cultivation tips and varieties

Aniseed comes from *Pimpinella anisum*, which is an annual needing a sunny position. The fruit will only ripen in a hot dry summer. Anise hyssop (*Agastache foeniculum*) is a hardy perennial that grows to about 1 metre (3 feet) and is happy in most soils. Star anise is the seed of *Illicum verum*, an evergreen tree mainly grown in China, but it is not suitable for growing for culinary purposes and should be bought specially for that purpose.

Best way to preserve, dry or store

The seeds should be harvested when they turn grey-green and then hung up until fully ripe. They can then be shaken out and stored in an airtight container. Anise hyssop (*Agastache foeniculum*) is grown mainly for decorative purposes and the flowers can be hung up and air dried.

Culinary and decorative uses

When used in moderation, aniseed is excellent in fish dishes and curries, giving a similar flavour to fennel. Star anise is an indispensable ingredient of Chinese five-spice powder. It is invaluable in small-scale decorative work, such as posies, wedding head-dresses or when decorating presents or other tiny items. Anise hyssop is a wonderfully aromatic plant which produces blue-purple flower spikes and gives a good smell and colour to dried flower arrangements.

Medicinal uses

Aniseed is used commercially in cough medicines and lozenges. The essential oil can be used in aromatherapy to ease coughs, colds and bronchitis, but take care when using it as it can sometimes irritate the skin.

History and myths

Aniseed was used in powders and potions by both the Egyptians and the Romans, and was said to ward off the Evil One. Star anise has been used by the Chinese for medicinal purposes for over 1000 years.

Piper nigrum
PEPPER

Pepper must be one of the best-known condiments, certainly in the Western world. You can buy black, white, pink and green peppercorns but they all come from this one plant. The berries are picked from the pepper vine while they are still green, then dried in the sun to produce black peppercorns. Green peppercorns are simply unripe berries, which may be dried, pickled or canned. Pink or red peppercorns are berries that have been allowed to ripen on the vine. White peppercorns are produced when these ripened pink berries are picked, soaked in brine and the outer skin is removed. Some companies are passing off the berries of a South American weed as pink peppercorns, so buy them from a reputable manufacturer – this weed has occasionally poisoned people.

Cultivation
The pepper plant grows in the hot jungle areas of Indonesia, Malaysia, Sri Lanka and India. The pepper vines are harvested by hand and women with baskets on their heads still pick much of the world's pepper crop.

Best way to preserve, dry or store
All pepper, whatever its colour, is best freshly milled, so always buy relatively small quantities of peppercorns and grind them as you need them. Ready-ground pepper should never be kept for long because it quickly loses its flavour.

Culinary and decorative uses
Many cooks automatically add ground pepper to every savoury dish they make, but some thought should go into its use because it can subtly alter the flavour of the dish. Black pepper can also be used as a sweet spice and is particularly effective with fresh strawberries – it brings out their flavour yet hides its own. There are few decorative uses for peppercorns because they are so small.

Medicinal uses
Black pepper essential oil is used in aromatherapy to treat chilblains, anaemia, sluggish digestion and general stiffness of the joints. It is also good for colds, flu and catarrh.

History and myths
Pepper has been a popular spice with many civilizations. The Romans used

it extensively because it was fairly cheap. During the Dark Ages in Britain, however, it was very expensive, although it became more easily available from the thirteenth century onwards. By the Middle Ages, low rents were often paid in inferior pepper – hence the expression 'a peppercorn rent'.

ROSEMARY

Rosmarinus officinalis
ROSEMARY
Rosemary is one of my favourite herbs and certainly one I would not want to be without. The long needle-like grey-green leaves look very attractive all year round, and particularly just after it has rained or in the early morning dew. The flowers are small and blue, and the scent is strongly balsamic.

Cultivation tips and varieties
Rosemary can be propagated from seed or cuttings taken in the spring.

Rosmarinus officinalis is a perennial shrub that likes a warm sheltered and well-drained position, and there are varieties that give blue, pink and white flowers, upright or prostrate plants.

Best way to preserve, dry or store
For culinary purposes, this herb can be picked fresh all year round, so there is no need to store it. However, it can save time to make rosemary butter in advance and keep it in the freezer until needed. For decorative use, rosemary branches can be picked at any time of year and hung up in a warm airy place to air dry. Their stems can also be placed in an equal mixture of glycerine and water to preserve them, but the needles will change colour.

Culinary and decorative uses
Rosemary is a very strong and pungent herb but, when used skilfully, it can give an unforgettable taste and aroma to a dish. It is often used with lamb but is also excellent with liver, sausages, pork and poultry. Rosemary can be very attractive when dried and used in decorative arrangements.

Medicinal uses
Rosemary has always been a valued herb for medicinal purposes, especially for its calming and antiseptic properties. Rosemary tea is good for nervous disorders and an infusion of the leaves is an excellent hair rinse and also a good footbath. Rosemary essential oil should not be used during pregnancy or by epileptics. It is particularly useful in the treatment of scalp conditions such as dandruff. It is also a natural insect repellent. Rosemary also helps to soothe muscular pain, combats fluid retention, poor circulation, headaches, stress-related disorders, mental fatigue and is said to enhance the memory.

History and myths
The Romans took rosemary with them to Europe and Britain, where it is said to grow best of all. In Tudor times it was an ingredient in many recipes and also had many medicinal and aromatic uses. It has long been associated with magic and is regarded as a sacred plant in many cultures.

Salvia officinalis
SAGE

The grey-green common sage is the best-known variety, but there are several others which are worth adding to your collection. Sage is invaluable as a culinary herb.

Cultivation tips and varieties
Sage is a hardy perennial which can either be sown from seed, which should be well-watered until germination takes place, or propagated from cuttings. It likes a sunny and well-drained position. The plants can become woody with age, so are best replaced every three of four years. Sage is a good companion plant to cabbages and carrots. Among the different sages that can be grown are the dark purple or red variety, *Salvia officinalis* 'Purpurascens', the very pretty pink and white variegated sage, *S. o.* 'Tricolor' and the golden variegated sage, *S.o.* 'Icterina'.

Best way to preserve, dry or store
Sage is best picked in late spring, but can be harvested all year round. It can be air dried in small bunches and then stored carefully in airtight containers when thoroughly dry. Sprays of the leaves can be wrapped in foil and frozen.

Culinary and decorative uses
Sage goes best with fatty foods, such as goose, duck and pork, and with oily

SAGE

fish. It also works well with cheese dishes and, indeed, some commercial cheeses in Britain and the US are flavoured with sage. It is good in stuffings. Dried sprigs of sage can be used in arrangements but they are fairly brittle.

Medicinal uses
Sage is considered to be a good cleanser of the blood, and sage tea is an excellent tonic and remedy for rheumatic pain. Two essential oils are made from sage. Common sage oil can be toxic and should only be used under the guidance of a professional aromatherapist; clary sage oil should never be used during pregnancy but at other times it is good for treating depression, kidney disorders, high blood pressure, throat infections and digestive disorders.

History and myths
Sage originates from the Mediterranean area and was taken to many parts of northern Europe by the Romans. It was used to cure all manner of ailments and was meant to prevent the ravages of time and promote eternal youth! The Egyptians used sage to improve their intellectual powers and to revive the brain after mental fatigue.

Satureia species
SAVORY

There are two varieties of savory – winter (*Satureia montana*) and summer (*S. hortensis*). They have very similar tastes (hot and spicy), fragrances and uses, but winter savory is a perennial with thin, small green leaves and summer savory is an annual with a bronze tint to the leaves, which are slightly larger than the winter variety.

Cultivation tips

Winter savory is best propagated by taking cuttings in the late spring, but it can also be grown from seed in drills and later planted out in the herb garden. Summer savory is grown from seed in its intended position; it is a good companion plant to broad (fava) beans. Both plants like a sunny position in a poor, dry soil.

Best way to preserve, dry or store

Both varieties of savory can be air dried in the usual manner, but winter savory has a better flavour for culinary purposes. Summer savory is best grown for inclusion in fresh and dried herb arrangements.

Culinary and decorative uses

Savory is particularly good with pulses and also other vegetables. It can be used in stews, stuffings and salads. Savory adds a nice aroma to dried arrangements and looks most effective when used in bundles rather than as individual wispy strands.

Medicinal uses

Both winter and summer savory have been used to aid digestion and soothe nausea. Savory essential oil is quite unsuitable for home use unless it is under the guidance of a professional aromatherapist.

History and myths

Savory originally came from southern Europe and was taken to Britain by the Romans. It was highly favoured for its spicy peppery taste and was also considered to be an aphrodisiac. Winter savory was used during Tudor times for low hedging in knot gardens.

Thymus vulgaris
THYME

Thyme is a small evergreen perennial shrub with small grey-green aromatic leaves and tiny white or purple flowers. There are many varieties, all of which are easy to grow and are a must in any well-stocked herb garden.

Cultivation tips and varieties

Common thyme, or *Thymus vulgaris,* is a perennial, as are the many other varieties available. All thymes can be grown from seed, cuttings or root division, but we have always found the latter two options to be most effective.

THYME

Among the varieties you can grow are lemon thyme (*T. citriodorus*), which I would not be without. Thyme is a good companion plant to cabbages, as it helps to repel cabbage root fly.

Best way to preserve, dry or store

The branches can be picked just before the flowers come into bloom, hung up to air dry and then stored in airtight containers in a warm airy place. Alternatively, you can freeze generous pinches of individual leaves with a little water in ice cube trays.

Culinary and decorative uses

Thyme is an ingredient of dried mixed herbs (Italian seasoning) and also bouquet garni. It is especially good in pâtés, pies, sauces and stuffings, and complements many vegetable and vegetarian dishes. Decoratively, it looks very attractive in clumps or bunches.

Medicinal uses

An infusion of thyme leaves makes an excellent mouth wash and can also be used to bathe infected wounds. Thyme essential oil should never be used during pregnancy. It should always be

SAVORY

used with care as it can be an irritant, but it treats many skin complaints such as acne, bruising, burns, cuts and infections. It can help poor circulation, sprains, sports injuries, infectious diseases and headaches and is also helpful for alleviating problems with the respiratory system.

History and myths
In Greek, thyme means to perfume, and the Egyptians used it in their embalming processes. In medieval England, thyme signified courage, long life and freedom from sickness, and sprigs of thyme were given to brave knights before they galloped off to the Crusades.

Vanilla planifolia
VANILLA
Vanilla pods or beans grow on a climbing orchid which is native to the coastline of South America. The pods are about 10cm (4 in) long and, once they have been dried, are dark brown or nearly black.

Cultivation
The plants from this member of the orchid family are trained to grow up poles and tree trunks. *Vanilla planifolia* grows throughout the tropics but the finest vanilla pods still come from Mexico.

Best way to preserve, dry or store
The pods are harvested when they are unripe. They are boiled and then packed tightly into containers, in which they turn their characteristic dark brown. The highest quality pods have a fine crystalline covering. Only buy a few vanilla pods at a time so they will not turn stale and store them in an airtight container at room temperature in a dark place.

Culinary and decorative uses
Vanilla is one of the most popular flavourings for sweet dishes such as ice cream and, although vanilla essence (extract) is a reasonable substitute, it is not as good as the real thing. Vanilla sugar can be easily made by burying one or two vanilla pods in a jar of sugar – this not only keeps the vanilla pod fresh but also flavours the sugar ready for use in sweet cookery. The pods have limited use for decorations and they are also expensive, but they can add an interesting shape and texture to arrangements of spices.

Medicinal uses
Perhaps because of its soothing and warm flavour, vanilla was once used to treat nervous conditions.

History and myths
Vanilla was first discovered by the Spanish in Mexico during the sixteenth century. The Aztecs used it to flavour chocolate drinks and the Spanish added it to sangria. It is also used in perfumes and pot pourris.

Zingiber officinale
GINGER
Ginger is associated with both sweet and savoury dishes and is one of the best-known spices. It is the rhizome, or root, that is used in cookery, whether fresh, dried, candied or crystallized.

Cultivation tips
The ginger plant is quite beautiful in its own right as a flower, and looks a little like a large lily. *Zingiber officinale* needs a warm humid climate and a great deal of water if it is to thrive. The plant has narrow spear-shaped leaves, thick woody stems and spikes of white or yellow flowers.

Best way to preserve, dry or store
The rhizomes of the ginger plant are harvested when they are at least one year old and are soaked in syrup, dried, powdered or sold fresh as green ginger. Fresh ginger should be stored in the refrigerator, while the dried or powdered forms should be kept in airtight containers.

Culinary and decorative uses
Ginger is easily obtained and is an inexpensive spice that has many uses; it can be added to curries and is often included in Chinese recipes. Drinks are among the most popular foodstuffs containing ginger flavourings – ginger beer, ginger ale and ginger wine. Decoratively, the dried root can be added to pot pourris or wired or glued into position on decorations.

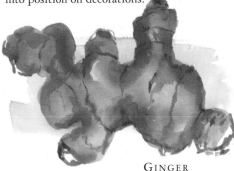

GINGER

Medicinal uses
During the Middle Ages, ginger was thought to protect against the plague. In aromatherapy, ginger essential oil is used to treat poor circulation, sprains and strains. It also eases catarrh, sinusitis, sore throats, travel sickness, colds and nervous exhaustion.

History and myths
Ginger is one of the oldest spices and is mentioned in many historical works. The Romans taxed ginger as well as tobacco and alcohol, and many cultures have used this spice in their cookery.

A FEAST
OF
HERBS AND SPICES

This section contains lots of recipes, using

herbs and spices, for soups and starters

(appetizers), fish dishes, meat and poultry

dishes, salads and vegetarian dishes,

desserts and drinks and, last but not least,

dips, sauces and oils.

CORIANDER (CILANTRO), CARROT AND GINGER SOUP

♣

This has always been a very popular summer soup with both my family and the guests who come on my courses. Its colour is very cheerful and makes a lovely contrast with many different styles of china. You can freeze this soup if you wish to make it in advance.

SERVES 4

25 g (1 oz/2 tbsp) butter

1 large onion, peeled and chopped

5-10 ml (1-2 tsp) fresh ginger, grated

1 litre (1¾ pints/4¼ cups) good chicken or strong vegetable stock

5 medium-sized carrots, peeled and chopped

15 ml (1 tbsp) fresh coriander leaves (cilantro), chopped

to garnish, coriander leaves and julienne sticks of carrot

Heat the butter, onion and ginger in a saucepan and cook for about 3-4 minutes or until the onion has softened. Add all the remaining ingredients except the fresh coriander (cilantro) and bring to the boil, then simmer until the carrots are tender (about 10-15 minutes). Add the coriander. Place the mixture in a food processor (in two batches, if necessary) and process until completely smooth. Chill in the refrigerator for several hours before serving. To serve, place in bowls and garnish each one with a sprig of coriander and a few carrot sticks in the centre.

GREEN GARDEN SOUP

♣

This is a delicious cold summer soup which can't fail to impress any health-conscious friends as it contains masses of vitamins and other nutrients. If you don't have this exact blend of greenery available then you can alter the recipe by substituting any other herb of your choice.

SERVES 4

2 litres (3½ pints/8½ cups) water

225 g (8 oz) fresh spinach, washed

100 g (4 oz/1½ cup) rocket (arugula) leaves, washed

4 spring onions (scallions), cleaned

30 ml (2 tbsp) fresh parsley, washed

30 ml (2 tbsp) fresh dill, washed

50 g (2 oz/1½ cups) watercress, washed

1 cucumber, washed and roughly chopped

30 ml (2 tbsp) fresh lime juice

15 ml (1 tbsp) fresh grapefruit juice

30 ml (2 tbsp) olive oil

750 ml (1¼ pints/3¼ cups) good chicken or strong vegetable stock

salt and pepper to taste

to garnish, nasturtium leaves and shreds of lime and grapefruit peel

Bring the water to the boil in a large saucepan and add the spinach, rocket (arugula) and chopped spring onions (scallions). Boil until the spinach wilts (probably about 1-1½ minutes), then drain very thoroughly and discard the water. Place the cooked spinach mixture in a food processor and add the parsley, dill and watercress. Process until smooth, then add the remaining ingredients and process again until smooth. Taste and adjust seasoning if necessary. Pour into a large bowl and cover, then chill for several hours before serving. Garnish each bowl with a nasturtium leaf and scatter with some shreds of lime and grapefruit peel.

·

*These soups have vivid colours and fresh flavours –
Coriander, Carrot and Ginger Soup (top),
Green Garden Soup (middle) and
Apple and Red Cabbage Soup (bottom).*

APPLE AND RED CABBAGE SOUP
♣

The colour of this soup is reason enough to make it, but it tastes wonderful, too. The tomato juice and Worcestershire sauce give it an added dimension.

SERVES 4

15 g (½ oz/1 tbsp) butter
15 ml (1 tbsp) water
3-4 spring onions (scallions), cleaned and finely chopped
1 medium-sized leek, cleaned and finely chopped
1-2 cloves garlic, peeled and chopped (optional)
1 litre (1¾ pint/4¼ cups) good chicken stock
1 medium-sized potato, peeled and chopped
1 large eating apple, peeled and chopped
225 g (8 oz/3 cups) red cabbage, shredded
120 ml (4 fl oz/½ cup) fresh tomato juice
5-10 ml (1-2 tsp) Worcestershire sauce
30 ml (2 tbsp) chopped chives
to garnish, herb or garlic croûtons and chopped chives

Basil and Honeydew Melon Soup is deliciously refreshing when served on a hot summer's day, and it also has a wonderfully delicate smell.

Melt the butter in a large saucepan and add the water, spring onions (scallions), leek and the garlic if you are using it. Cook until the leek and onions are tender (about 5 minutes). Add the remaining ingredients, except for the chives, and bring the mixture to the boil, then simmer for about 20-30 minutes or until the potato is tender. Add the chives for the last couple of minutes. Process thoroughly in a food processor until smooth, then reheat gently before serving. To serve, pour into warmed bowls and garnish with herb or garlic croûtons and more chopped fresh chives.

BASIL AND HONEYDEW MELON SOUP
♣

Melon is a very popular starter (appetizer) but this way of serving it makes a lovely change. Although it may seem unusual to have a melon soup it is quite delicious.

SERVES 4

2 large ripe honeydew melons
juice and grated zest of 1 large orange
30 ml (2 tbsp) sweet white vermouth
30 ml (2 tbsp) fromage frais
15 ml (1 tbsp) grated fresh ginger
15 ml (1 tbsp) chopped fresh basil
salt and pepper to taste
to garnish, grated orange zest and fresh basil leaves

Cut the melons in half and, using a spoon or melon baller, scrape out the seeds and discard. Remove the flesh and place in a food processor. Add all the other ingredients and blend until really smooth. Refrigerate for several hours before serving. Serve cold, garnished with grated orange zest and fresh basil leaves.

When served with a mixed salad and crusty French bread,
Spicy Baked Goats' Cheese, with its accompanying spiced
apple sauce, makes an unusual light lunch.

SPICY BAKED GOATS' CHEESE
♣

Goats' cheese is now easily available in most large
supermarkets or small specialist shops and it tastes delicious
in this crunchy coating. This quantity could serve four as a
starter (appetizer) or two as a light lunch.

SERVES 4

5 ml (1 tsp) coarsely ground black pepper

60 ml (4 tbsp) wholemeal (whole-wheat) breadcrumbs

225 g (8 oz) wheel of goats' cheese

30 ml (2 tbsp) virgin olive oil

50 g (2 oz/¹/₄ cup) lightly stewed apple

10 ml (2 tsp) demerara or light brown sugar (optional)

2.5 ml (¹/₂ tsp) ground mixed spice (apple pie spice)

Mix the black pepper with the breadcrumbs and place in a wide bowl. Pour the olive oil into a wide bowl. Divide the cheese into four portions and dip each one first into the olive oil and then into the breadcrumbs, making sure that they have completely covered the surface of the cheese. Place on a dish and chill in the refrigerator. Meanwhile, place the stewed apple in a saucepan and add the ground mixed spice (apple pie spice), plus the demerara or brown sugar if you are using it. Warm the sauce through to blend the flavours and place on one side to cool. Pre-heat the oven to 240°C (475°F/Gas Mark 9). Place the cheese portions on a lightly greased baking sheet and bake for about 10 minutes or until lightly browned. The accompanying apple sauce can be served warm or cold. Arrange each piece of cheese on a small plate with a sprig of watercress and a spoonful of the apple sauce and serve immediately.

SPICED GUACAMOLE WITH HERBY PITTA BREAD

♣

This is always very popular and its flavours are complemented nicely by the herby pitta bread

SERVES 8

FOR GUACAMOLE
—
4 avocados

1 large clove garlic, peeled and finely chopped

1 onion, peeled and finely chopped

1 fresh chilli (chili pepper), finely chopped

juice of 1 fresh lime

5–6 drops Tabasco sauce, or to taste

salt and pepper to taste

2 large ripe tomatoes

FOR HERBY PITTA BREADS
—
100 g (4 oz/¹/₂ cup) butter

10 ml (2 tsp) finely chopped fresh parsley

10 ml (2 tsp) finely chopped fresh chives

10 ml (2 tsp) finely chopped fresh tarragon

10 ml (2 tsp) finely chopped fresh chervil

8 white or wholemeal (whole-wheat) pitta breads

Cut the avocados in half and remove the stones (pits). Scoop out all the flesh. Place in a bowl and add all the other ingredients except the tomatoes. Mash together well. Remove the skin from the tomatoes by leaving them in boiling water for a few seconds and then peel off the skin. Cut into quarters, remove the juice and seeds and discard. Chop the tomato flesh and stir into the mixture. Place the guacamole in the refrigerator until required. Stir the mixture well before serving if the surface has discoloured.

To make the herby pitta breads, let the butter soften and then cream in the finely chopped herbs. Leave the butter to stand for a couple of hours to allow the flavours to develop, then slice the pitta breads halfway across their width and spread the butter inside each pocket. Warm the bread through in a pre-heated oven, at 375°C (190°F/Gas Mark 5) for 5 minutes and serve immediately.

CHICKEN AND TARRAGON MOUSSE

♣

If you have a food processor you will be amazed at how easy this recipe is to make. You can make the mousse in advance as it will keep well in the refrigerator for a couple of days.

SERVES 8

50 g (2 oz/4 tbsp) butter

30 ml (2 tbsp) sunflower oil

1 medium-sized cooking apple, peeled and chopped

2 medium-sized onions, peeled and chopped

450 g (1 lb/2 cups) cream cheese

225 g (8 oz) pork sausagemeat

225 g (8 oz) chicken livers

120 ml (4 fl oz/¹/₂ cup) Calvados

5 ml (1 tsp) dried tarragon

10 ml (2 tsp) salt

10 ml (2 tsp) freshly ground black pepper

40 g (1¹/₂ oz/¹/₃ cup) walnuts, shelled

to garnish, sprigs of fresh herbs or apple slices

Melt the butter and half the oil in a saucepan, then add the onions and apple. Cook for about 10 minutes or until they are soft and transparent. Purée in a food processor, then add the cream cheese and process again. Using the remaining oil, thoroughly cook the sausagemeat and chicken livers, then pour the Calvados into one side of the pan and ignite it to burn off the alcohol. Blow out the flames and add the contents of the pan to the apple and onion mixture in the food processor and process until smooth. Add the herbs and seasoning and process again. Add the walnuts and process briefly. Place the mixture in an oiled loaf tin (bread pan) or dish and refrigerate. When it is chilled and ready to serve, garnish with sprigs of fresh herbs or slices of fresh apple, dipped in lemon juice to prevent them turning brown.

———— · ————

Opposite: Chicken and Tarragon Mousse (left) is quick to make. If serving the Spiced Guacamole (right) as a dip, cut the pitta bread into fingers.

Both these fish dishes are unusual and good to eat –
Smoked Salmon Pasta, flavoured with dill (right) and
Herby Lettuce Parcels Filled with Sea Bass (bottom left).

· · ·

SMOKED SALMON PASTA
♣

This makes a delicious light lunch. It is a treat at any time
of year but, if served with a salad, is an ideal summer dish.

SERVES 4

300 ml (½ pint/1¼ cups) double (heavy) cream

60 ml (4 tbsp/¼ cup) fromage frais

25 g (1 oz/2 tbsp) butter

salt and pepper

225-275 g (8-10 oz) smoked salmon

30 ml (2 tbsp) corn oil

700 g (1½ lb) fresh tagliatelle or fettuccine

60 ml (4 tbsp) finely chopped fresh dill

Heat the cream in a saucepan until it has reduced a little, then whisk in the fromage frais. Continue whisking until the mixture thickens up a little, then add the butter, and salt and pepper to taste, and cook for a further 2 minutes. Chop the smoked salmon and place about a quarter to one side for garnishing, plus a few sprigs of the dill. Add the corn oil to a large saucepan of salted boiling water and cook the pasta. Drain well and place in a large warmed bowl, add the cream sauce, smoked salmon and dill and stir well. Divide the mixture between four warmed plates and sprinkle with the remaining smoked salmon and chopped dill before serving immediately.

HERBY LETTUCE PARCELS (PACKAGES) FILLED WITH SEA BASS

♣

If it is difficult to obtain sea bass you can use cod instead for this recipe. Wrapping food in lettuce leaves instead of pastry is popular in several cuisines and can reduce the number of calories in a dish.

SERVES 4

4 x 175 g (6 oz) sea bass steaks
8 large crisp lettuce leaves

FOR THE STUFFING
—
2 medium-sized onions, peeling
450 g (1 lb) mushrooms
50 g (2 oz/4 tbsp) butter
salt and pepper
5-10 ml (1-2 tsp) white wine vinegar

FOR THE SAUCE
—
60 g (2½ oz/5 tbsp) butter
1 medium-sized onion, peeled and finely chopped
120 ml (4 fl oz/½ cup) fish stock, reduced
20 ml (4 tsp) white wine vinegar
240 ml (8 fl oz/1 cup) double (heavy) cream
60 ml (4 tbsp/½ cup) chopped fresh mixed herbs
salt and pepper
to garnish, 4 sprigs of fresh herbs

Growing your own herbs and then drying them for use during the winter is very easy and tremendously satisfying. Tie them in small bunches and leave to air dry on a wire rack.

First make the stuffing by chopping the onion and mushrooms separately. Melt the 50 g (2 oz/4 tbsp) butter in a pan and sauté the onion until transparent, then add the mushrooms, vinegar, salt and pepper. Reduce the heat and cook for 10-15 minutes or until all the liquid has evaporated, then remove from the heat and set aside. Bring a large saucepan of water to the boil and blanch the lettuce leaves in it until they are limp. Drain carefully and dry gently with a clean tea towel. Season the fish steaks with salt and pepper and make a pocket in each one by cutting three-quarters of the way through it from top to bottom with a sharp knife. Fill each one with a quarter of the stuffing mixture. Wrap two lettuce leaves around each steak to make a neat parcel (package). Place the parcels in a vegetable steamer and steam over a pan of boiling water for about 10 minutes.

To prepare the sauce, heat 25 g (1 oz/2 tbsp) of the butter in a pan, add the chopped onion and sauté for a couple of minutes. Add the fish stock and vinegar and whisk the ingredients together. Add the cream and herbs and continue to cook over a high heat until the sauce is reduced by about one-third. Then whisk in the remaining butter, adding a small piece at a time. Season with salt and pepper to taste.

To serve, pour a quarter of the sauce on each warmed plate and place the well-drained lettuce parcel carefully in the middle. Garnish each parcel with a small sprig of fresh herbs.

43

HALIBUT WITH A TARRAGON MARINADE
♣

Halibut and tarragon make excellent partners, but be sure to use French rather than Russian tarragon because the flavour is far superior. This dish is delicious served with tiny new potatoes, mange-tout (snow peas) and baby carrots.

SERVES 6

juice and grated zest of 2 lemons

15 ml (1 tbsp) French mustard

45 ml (3 tbsp) chopped fresh tarragon

30 ml (2 tbsp) chopped chives

30 ml (2 tbsp) virgin olive oil

salt and black pepper

6 x 225 g (8 oz) halibut steaks

to garnish, lemon twists and sprigs of tarragon

Combine the lemon juice and zest, mustard, herbs, olive oil and seasoning in a bowl or in a food processor until thoroughly blended. Place the fish steaks in a shallow dish, pour over the mixture and marinate for 2-3 hours. Pre-heat the grill (broiler) to maximum heat and grill (broil) the steaks for about 5 minutes on each side, then check that they are completely cooked. Serve garnished with twists of lemon and sprigs of tarragon.

Halibut with a Tarragon Marinade is a wonderful dish for a summer's day, and is equally good served with steamed baby vegetables or a simple mixed salad.

—————— • ——————

FRENCH TARRAGON

SCALLOP AND HERB SALAD
♣

This warm salad is another wonderful idea for a summer lunch. It has become a firm favourite in my family because it is looks as lovely as it tastes.

SERVES 4

FOR THE SALAD

3 ripe tomatoes
60 ml (4 tbsp) olive oil
1 small onion, peeled and very finely chopped
30 ml (2 tbsp) fresh lime or lemon juice
salt and pepper
30 ml (2 tbsp) finely chopped mixed fresh herbs
red and green lettuce leaves of your choice

FOR THE SCALLOPS

450 g (1 lb) scallops
30 ml (2 tbsp) olive oil
to garnish, finely chopped fresh herbs

To make the salad: Skin the tomatoes by leaving them in boiling water for a few seconds, then remove them and peel off the skin. Cut into quarters and remove the juice and seeds and discard. Chop the remaining flesh and place on one side until needed. Place the 60 ml (4 tbsp) olive oil in a saucepan and sauté the onion until soft and transparent. Add the lime or lemon juice, some salt and pepper, the mixed fresh herbs and the chopped tomato. Mix together well. Shred as much lettuce as you wish to use and mix the two colours together. Divide between four plates and pour over half the salad dressing.

To cook the scallops: Cut the scallops in half if they are particularly large, then sauté them in the 30 ml (2 tbsp) olive oil for 3-4 minutes. Add the remaining salad dressing and stir well. Divide the scallops, in their dressing, between the four plates and garnish each one with a sprinkling of finely chopped fresh herbs. Serve immediately.

If you're looking for a simple but spectacular dish for a special occasion, this warm Scallop and Herb Salad may be the answer. Serve it as soon as the scallops are cooked.

———————— · ————————

SPICED PRAWN (SHRIMP) SALAD

♣

The flavour of prawns (shrimp) is really enhanced when mixed with spices – in this case sesame oil and a little allspice. The sesame oil has a very strong flavour so you may wish to reduce the amount slightly if you find it too over powering.

SERVES 4

500 g (18 oz) king prawns (jumbo shrimp)
100 g (4 oz) mange-tout (snow peas), trimmed
1 medium-sized mango
freshly ground allspice
120 ml (4 tbsp/¹/₂ cup) fresh basil leaves
30 ml (2 tbsp/¹/₄ cup) fresh lemon or lime juice
45 ml (3 tbsp/¹/₃ cup) olive oil
15 ml (1 tbsp) sesame oil
mixed lettuce leaves, including oak leaf and radicchio
to garnish, sesame seeds

Remove the shells from the prawns (shrimp) if necessary. Lightly boil the mange-tout (snow peas) for a couple of minutes, drain into a colander and refresh under cold running water until cold. Peel and stone (pit) the mango and chop the flesh roughly. Place the mango, a little allspice, basil leaves and lime or lemon juice in a food processor and blend until smooth. Slowly add the olive and sesame oils and process again until completely blended. Arrange the lettuces on four plates and place the prawns and mange-tout on top of the leaves. Pour over the dressing and scatter sesame seeds on top as a garnish.

MACE AND NUTMEG

SMOKED MACKEREL WITH A SPICED CUCUMBER SAUCE

♣

Smoked mackerel is an inexpensive fish with an excellent flavour. This dish can be served as a starter (appetizer) or, if you add plenty of salads and wholemeal (whole-wheat) rolls, makes a terrific lunch.

SERVES 4

3 large cucumbers
2 medium-sized onions, peeled
salt
240 ml (8 fl oz/1 cup) dry white wine
480 ml (16 fl oz/2 cups) cider vinegar
¹/₂ nutmeg, grated
5 ml (1 tsp) black peppercorns
2 blades mace
4 fresh smoked mackerel fillets

Peel the cucumbers carefully with a cannelling knife, paring the skin into long narrow strips. Tie them into knots and put to one side to use as a garnish. Slice the onions and cucumbers finely, place the slices in a shallow dish and sprinkle with salt. Cover and leave in a refrigerator overnight. Before using, rinse well to remove the salt and liquid. Cook the cucumber and onion slices in a large saucepan for about 30 minutes, then strain carefully, retaining all the liquid. Pour half this liquid into another saucepan and add the wine, vinegar and seasonings. Simmer for about 5 minutes, then strain the liquid into a jug and chill. Serve the mackerel cold, with some of the chilled sauce placed on the side of each plate and garnished with the knots of cucumber peel.

_____ · _____

Opposite: *When preparing dishes like Spiced Prawn (shrimp) Salad (bottom) and Smoked Mackerel with a Spiced Cucumber Sauce (top) it pays to use the best quality ingredients.*

SWORDFISH WITH SPICED ORANGES
♣

Swordfish has a pleasing meaty texture and has recently become easier to find in shops and supermarkets. This recipe was given to me by a friend after I raved about it at one of her dinner parties, although I've made a few changes to it.

SERVES 4

3 large oranges
2.5 ml (½ tsp) ground allspice
15 ml (1 tbsp) Grand Marnier
salt and black pepper
4 swordfish steaks
100 g (4 oz/½ cup) butter
about 175 ml (6 fl oz/¾ cup) fish stock, well reduced
juice from 1 orange
to garnish, slices or twists of orange and sprigs of watercress

Peel the three oranges and carefully separate the segments, keeping them as intact as possible. Peel or cut away all the skin and any remaining pith with a sharp knife. Combine the allspice and Grand Marnier in a bowl, add the orange segments and mix gently. Leave to absorb the flavours for about 1-2 hours. When ready, pre-heat the grill (broiler) to maximum heat, sprinkle a little salt and pepper over each steak and spread on half the butter. Grill (broil) the steaks for about 3-4 minutes on each side and baste with the pan juices so the fish doesn't dry out.

Meanwhile, in a saucepan, mix together the fish stock, orange juice and any liquid left in the bowl containing the orange segments. Bring to the boil and reduce by about one-third, then whisk in the remaining butter, carefully add the orange segments and cook for no more than 1 minute. Place a swordfish steak on each warmed plate and cover with some of the sauce. Garnish with slices or twists of orange and a few sprigs of watercress.

If you have never tried cooking swordfish, why not experiment by making Swordfish with Spiced Oranges. It's a fish dish with a delicious difference.

———— • ————

CELEBRATION HAM WITH A MUSTARD AND BASIL CRUST

♣

This herby crust gives the ham a lovely flavour. The ham is delicious served with Sweet Basil Sauce (see below) or perhaps an apple-based herb jelly.

4.5 kg (10 lb) ham joint

FOR THE MARINADE

3 small onions, peeled and chopped
1 garlic clove, peeled and finely chopped
300 ml (½ pint/1¼ cups) red wine
300 ml (½ pint/1¼ cups) cider or water
large handful basil leaves, chopped

FOR THE CRUST

75 ml (5 tbsp) fresh basil leaves, chopped
175-200 g (6-7 oz) jar wholegrain mustard

To make the marinade, place all the ingredients in a bowl and mix together thoroughly. Place the ham in a very large mixing bowl and pour over the marinade, basting it all over the joint to ensure it is evenly distributed. Cover and chill in the refrigerator for several hours, turning the ham joint in the liquid marinade frequently. Ideally, the ham should be left to marinate for 24 hours.

Pre-heat the oven to 180°C (350°F/Gas Mark 4). Place the ham in a baking dish and pour over the marinade. Roast in the oven for 2 hours or so (allow 20 minutes per 450 kg/1 lb) or until the juices run nearly clear from the joint when a skewer is pressed into the flesh. Do not overcook the meat at this stage. Remove the ham from the oven, pour off the marinade and discard it. Turn up the heat of the oven to 220°C (425°F/Gas Mark 7). Strip off the skin. Mix together the mustard and basil leaves and spread over the surface of the joint. Replace the ham in the baking dish and replace it in the oven. Cook until the mustard mixture has dried out and formed a crust on the surface of the ham (about 20 minutes). Remove the ham from the oven and serve hot or cold with the Sweet Basil Sauce.

The herby flavour of Celebration Ham with a Mustard and Basil Crust makes a pleasant change from cloves and brown sugar as a decoration. Serve it hot or cold.

·

SWEET BASIL SAUCE

♣

This sauce can be made well in advance and kept covered in the refrigerator. It is the perfect accompaniment to the Celebration Ham.

60 ml (4 tbsp/¼ cup) wholegrain mustard
45 ml (3 tbsp/¼ cup) demerara or light brown sugar
30 ml (2 tbsp) red wine or cider vinegar
5 ml (1 tsp) English mustard powder
75 ml (5 tbsp/⅓ cup) sunflower oil
45 ml (3 tbsp/¼ cup) fresh basil, finely chopped

Place all the ingredients, except the oil and basil, in a food processor or blender and process well until smooth. Add the oil in a steady stream as though you were making mayonnaise, and process until the sauce is thick and very smooth. Stir in the basil by hand and pour into a serving bowl. Chill in a refrigerator for 2-3 hours before serving.

GRANNY'S HERBY MEAT LOAF
♣

This recipe is a prime example of the superior flavour fresh herbs have over dried ones. It has always been a family favourite even with the children.

SERVES 8

15-20 cm (6-8 inch) piece of day-old French or other bread
60 ml (4 tbsp/¼ cup) fresh thyme leaves
125 ml (8 tbsp/½ cup) fresh basil leaves
60 g (2 oz/1 cup) fresh parsley leaves
1 kg (2¼ lb) very lean beef, minced (ground)
700 g (1½ lb) lean pork, minced (ground)
1 large onion, peeled and chopped
3 medium eggs
30 ml (2 tbsp) Worcestershire sauce
30 ml (2 tbsp) grated Cheddar cheese
5 ml (1 tsp) hot chilli (chili) sauce
45 ml (3 tbsp) tomato ketchup (catsup)
salt and black pepper

Roughly chop the piece of French bread and process in a food processor until it turns to breadcrumbs. You can use any other leftover bread instead – this is a good way to use up crusts or the heels of loaves. Empty the crumbs into a large mixing bowl. Process all the herbs until they are very finely chopped, then add them to the mixing bowl. Add all the other ingredients and mix together very thoroughly. The first time you make this recipe you might wish to test the seasoning by frying a teaspoon of the mixture and tasting it; you can then add more Worcestershire or hot chilli (chili) sauce, salt or pepper as needed.

Pre-heat the oven to 180°C (350°F/Gas Mark 4). Butter or oil the inside of a large meat loaf tin (bread pan) or deep-sided casserole dish and gently pack the mixture into it. Press the top down firmly and bake in the oven for about 1½ hours or until cooked. Remove from the oven and allow to stand for several minutes, then drain off any excess fat or juices. Turn out on to a large platter and serve surrounded by vegetables or bunches of herbs.

CHICKEN WITH FIGS AND ALLSPICE
♣

This gives chicken an unusual twist. It has a wonderfully rich sauce, so is perfect with steamed vegetables.

SERVES 4

4-5 dried figs
30 ml (2 tbsp) tawny port
salt and black pepper
2.5 ml (½ tsp) ground allspice
90 g (3½ oz/7 tbsp) butter
30 ml (2 tbsp) water
900 g (2 lb) chicken breast fillets, skinned
30 ml (2 tbsp) red wine vinegar
1 small onion, peeled and finely chopped
240 ml (8 fl oz/1 cup) double (heavy) cream
to garnish, sprigs of parsley or other fresh herbs

Trim the stalks (stems) off the figs and chop the figs roughly. Place them in a dish, pour over the port and leave to marinate for about 1 hour. Place in a saucepan and add a pinch of salt, the allspice, 15 g (½ oz/1 tbsp) of the butter and the water. Simmer gently for 20 minutes or until the figs have absorbed most of the liquid. Purée in a food processor with another 30 g (1 oz/2 tbsp) of the butter and put to one side. Slice across the chicken breasts diagonally to make 12-mm (½-in) thick slices and sauté the pieces in another 45 g (1½ oz/3 tbsp) of the butter until they are just cooked. Place on an ovenproof plate and cover, then keep warm until you finish the sauce. Deglaze the pan with the vinegar and onion and the final 15 g (½ oz/1 tbsp) of butter, stir well and cook for 2-3 minutes or until the onion has softened and is transparent. Add the cream and boil for a minute, then add the fig purée and season with salt and pepper. Pass the sauce through a fine sieve (strainer) and reheat in a clean pan before serving.

———— · ————

Chicken with Figs and Allspice (bottom) and Lamb with a Basil and Apple Sauce (top), the recipe for which is on page 54.

DUCK WITH MINT AND GRAPEFRUIT
♣

Most people are used to eating duck with cherries or orange, so this combination comes as a pleasant change, and the fresh flavours help to cut through the richness of the duck.

SERVES 4

2 x 1.3 kg (3 lb) ducks, plucked and drawn
50 g (2 oz/4 tbsp) butter, melted
100 g (4 oz/1 cup) plain (all-purpose) flour
480 ml (16 fl oz/2 cups) water
240 ml (8 fl oz/1 cup) white wine
30 ml (2 tbsp) sweet sherry or Madeira
120 ml (4 fl oz/¹/₂ cup) Cointreau
30 ml (2 tbsp) brandy
120 ml (4 fl oz/¹/₂ cup) grapefruit juice
30 ml (2 tbsp) finely chopped fresh mint leaves
salt and black pepper
425 g (15 oz) can grapefruit segments
to garnish, sprigs of fresh mint

MINT

Duck with Mint and Grapefruit is another recipe with an interesting twist. The freshness of the mint and grapefruit is a good contrast to the rich duck meat.

Pre-heat the oven to 220°C (425°F/Gas Mark 7). Wash and dry the ducks and place in a baking dish. Bake in the oven for 1 hour, brushing the ducks frequently with the melted butter. Remove the ducks from the dish. Reduce the oven heat to 190°C (375°F/Gas Mark 5). Strain off all the fat from the dish into a container and keep to one side, but leave the juices in the dish. Place it on top of the oven and heat until the juices turn golden brown but do not

burn, then take off the heat and add 120 ml (4 fl oz/½ cup) of the fat you strained off. Sift in the flour and stir well. Return to the heat and stir the mixture until it turns a dark golden brown but does not burn.

Add the water, wine, sherry, Cointreau, brandy and grapefruit juice and stir until the sauce boils and thickens. Add the finely chopped mint leaves, salt and plenty of black pepper. Place the ducks in a large casserole dish, pour over the sauce and bake in the

oven for about 1½ hours or until the ducks are tender.

Place the grapefruit segments, plus their juice, in a saucepan and heat through. Remove the ducks from the baking dish and arrange on a large serving dish. Pour over the sauce and arrange the grapefruit segments beside the ducks. Decorate with a sprig of fresh mint and serve immediately. Alternatively you can slice the ducks in half lengthwise before arranging on the serving dish.

LAMB WITH A BASIL AND APPLE SAUCE

♣

You may automatically think of pork with apple sauce but this combination works equally well.

SERVES 4

120 ml (4 fl oz/¹/₂ cup) sunflower oil,
plus extra for brushing

2 small eating apples

125 ml (8 tbsp/1 cup) fresh basil leaves

1 clove garlic, peeled

120 ml (4 fl oz/¹/₂ cup) cider vinegar

15 ml (1 tbsp) fresh lime or lemon juice

4 leg of lamb steaks

black pepper

to garnish, sprigs of fresh basils or watercress

Peel the apples and remove the cores and pips (seeds), then chop them roughly and place in a food processor with the basil, garlic, vinegar and lemon or lime juice. Process until smooth, then add the oil in a steady stream while the processor is running until the mixture is smooth and all the ingredients are incorporated. Brush the lamb steaks with the extra sunflower oil and grind some black pepper over each one. Place under a pre-heated grill (broiler) on full heat and cook for about 5 minutes on each side or until the steaks are very slightly pink in the middle. Place a steak on each warmed plate with a spoonful of the basil and apple sauce and garnish with a sprig of fresh basil or watercress.

You can use lamb chops instead of steaks when making Lamb with a Basil and Apple Sauce. Serve with tiny new potatoes and a selection of steamed baby vegetables.

———— • ————

If your family and friends enjoy eating roast meat,
try serving them Pork with Rhubarb and Cinnamon for a
delicious change, and wait for the compliments to flow!

·

PORK WITH RHUBARB AND CINNAMON
♣

This is a terrific dish which always draws favourable
comments from guests. It may sound an unusual combination
but it's one that works very well.

SERVES 6

15 g (¹/₂ oz/1 tbsp) butter

15 ml (1 tbsp) sunflower oil

1.3 kg (3 lb) pork loin joint

120 ml (4 fl oz/¹/₂ cup) Madeira

480 ml (16 fl oz/2 cups) chicken stock

450 g (1 lb) rhubarb

75 g (3 oz/¹/₃ cup) demerara or light brown sugar

60 ml (2 fl oz/¹/₄ cup) water

10 ml (2 tsp) ground cinnamon

10 ml (2 tsp) fresh ginger, grated

15 ml (1 tbsp) double (heavy) cream

salt and black pepper

to garnish, cinnamon sticks and sprigs of watercress or parsley

Pre-heat the oven to 180°C (350°F/Gas Mark 4). Heat the butter and oil in a large ovenproof dish on the top of the oven, then put in the pork loin joint and brown on all sides. Remove the pork and strain off any excess fat and discard. Add the Madeira and chicken stock and bring to the boil, stirring well. Chop the rhubarb into small chunks and place in a separate pan with the sugar and water. Cover and cook for 8-10 minutes or until soft. Stir in the cinnamon and ginger, then add to the sauce in the ovenproof dish and stir well. Replace the pork in the dish, spoon some of the sauce over it and bake in the oven for about 1¹/₂ hours or until the pork is cooked. Remove the pork, place on a warmed dish and leave in a warm place. Pour the cream into the sauce and boil until the sauce has reduced by about one-third. Check the seasoning and, if necessary, add more ginger, cinnamon, salt or pepper. To serve, carve the pork into slices and arrange on a large serving dish or individual plates, pour over the sauce and garnish with sprigs of watercress or parsley and some cinnamon sticks.

GADO-GADO

♣

I first tasted this dish in a Balinese restaurant in London and loved it. I have altered this recipe over the years but it is still one of my favourite dishes.

SERVES 4

175 g (6 oz) white cabbage
1 onion, peeled and finely chopped
1 clove garlic, peeled and finely chopped
15 ml (1 tbsp) peanut or walnut oil
2.5 ml (½ tsp) chilli (chili) powder
10 ml (2 tsp) grated fresh ginger
30 ml (2 tbsp) crunchy peanut butter
15 ml (1 tbsp) hot water
salt and black pepper
4 hard-boiled eggs, shelled
175 g (6 oz/1½ cups) bean sprouts
175 g (6 oz/1 heaped cup) cucumber, peeled and cubed
50 g (2 oz/⅓ cup) salted peanuts

Shred the white cabbage and blanch in boiling water for a few minutes, then drain and cool under cold running water. Fry the onion and garlic in the nut oil for a few minutes, then add the chilli (chili) powder and ginger and cook for another 2 minutes. Add the peanut butter and hot water to give a creamy consistency – add more hot water if necessary. Season to taste, then leave to cool.

Cut the hard-boiled eggs into quarters lengthwise. Mix together the bean sprouts, white cabbage and cucumber, arrange on serving plates and pour over some of the sauce. Cut the hard-boiled eggs into quarters lengthwise and place on the salad, then scatter some peanuts on top and serve.

SPICY BEAN SALAD

♣

This makes a great vegetarian lunch with some green salad and lovely crusty bread. Unless you regularly cook your own dried pulses it is easiest and quickest to use canned beans for this recipe, and you can alter the varieties to include your favourites if you wish.

SERVES 4

15 ml (1 tbsp) chopped fresh basil leaves
30 ml (2 tbsp) lemon juice, freshly squeezed
10 ml (2 tsp) grated fresh ginger
large pinch of ground cinnamon
large pinch of ground coriander seed
90 ml (3 fl oz/⅓ cup) olive oil
175 g (6 oz/1 cup) red kidney beans, cooked
175 g (6 oz/1 cup) borlotti beans, cooked
175 g (6 oz/1 cup) chick peas (garbanzo beans), cooked
1 medium onion, peeled
75 g (3 oz) mange-tout (snow peas)
4 ripe tomatoes
lettuce

In a bowl, mix together the basil leaves, lemon juice, ginger, cinnamon, coriander and olive oil. Add the drained beans and mix well. Finely chop the onion and add it to the salad. Boil the mange-tout (snow peas) for a couple of minutes, then rinse them well under cold running water. Chop them roughly and stir them into the bean mixture, then cover and chill it for at least 2 hours before serving.

To serve, arrange some of the lettuce leaves on each plate and arrange some of the bean salad in the middle of the lettuce. Slice or quarter the tomatoes and scatter some over or around each plate of salad.

———— · ————

Opposite: Both the Gado-Gado (bottom) and Spicy Bean Salad (top) can be served as dishes in their own right or as separate salads for a large buffet meal.

HERBED CREAM CHEESE

♣

This cheese recipe can be used as a sandwich filler, or with plenty of salad and fresh crusty bread for a delicious lunch. You can also dilute the mixture with a little milk to make an interesting dip.

SERVES 4

1 clove garlic, peeled
100 g (4 oz/¹/₂ cup) cream cheese
100 g (4 oz/¹/₂ cup) ricotta cheese
120 ml (4 fl oz/¹/₂ cup) fromage frais
15 ml (1 tbsp) finely chopped fresh parsley
15 ml (1 tbsp) finely chopped fresh chives
15 ml (1 tbsp) finely chopped fresh marjoram
15 ml (1 tbsp) finely chopped fresh tarragon
15 ml (1 tbsp) finely chopped fresh basil
salt and black pepper

Mince or crush the clove of garlic, then combine it with all the other ingredients in a food processor and process until smooth. Alternatively, you can mix the ingredients together by hand in a large bowl. Refrigerate until needed.

You can experiment with the herbs that go into Herbed Cream Cheese, choosing whatever you have available at the time, just as long as they are fresh and not dried.

COURGETTE (ZUCCHINI) AND HERB FILO PARCELS

♣

Filo pastry is much easier to use than everyone imagines, so be brave and have a go if you have never tried it before. On the other hand, if you are already a convert then this is another recipe to add to your collection.

SERVES 6

75 g (3 oz/¹/₃ cup) pine kernels

5 medium-sized courgettes (zucchini)

salt and black pepper

1 small onion, peeled

30 ml (2 tbsp) olive oil

1 clove garlic, peeled and crushed

125 ml (8 tbsp/1 cup) fresh basil leaves

45 ml (3 tbsp) finely chopped fresh parsley

60 ml (2 fl oz/¹/₄ cup) dry white wine

2 medium eggs

50 g (2 oz/¹/₂ cup) Parmesan cheese, grated

75 g (3 oz/¹/₂ cup) Feta cheese, crumbled

6 sheets filo pastry

100 g (4 oz/¹/₂ cup) melted butter

Courgette (zucchini) and Herb Filo Parcels prove that vegetarian food doesn't have to be boring. Serve with red and yellow cherry tomatoes for extra colour and taste.

•

You must keep the filo pastry covered with a clean damp cloth whenever you are not actually working with it, as it dries out and cracks very quickly.

Pre-heat the oven to 180°C (350°F/Gas Mark 4). Roast the pine kernels for 5-10 minutes, then chop them finely. Grate the unpeeled courgettes (zucchini), using the largest size hole on the grater or processor. Place in a shallow dish, sprinkle with salt and leave for 30-45 minutes, then drain and squeeze any excess liquid out of them. Chop the onion and sauté it in the olive oil for 2 minutes. Add the courgettes and plenty of black pepper and sauté for another 3-4 minutes. Add the garlic, basil, parsley and white wine, cover and cook for about 3 minutes. Remove from the heat.

Break the eggs into a bowl and beat them, add the cheeses and then stir in the cooked vegetables. Adjust the seasoning if necessary. Take a sheet of filo pastry and brush half its upper surface with melted butter, then fold over the unbuttered half to make a square.

Place about 30 ml (2 tbsp) of the vegetable mixture in the top left corner of the filo pastry and fold the bottom right corner over it to make a triangle. Fold in the sides and brush them with melted butter to make them stick together. Place the filo triangle on a buttered baking sheet and brush the pastry with more melted butter, then cover with a clean damp cloth while you make the next triangle. Meanwhile, reheat the oven to 240°C (475°F/Gas Mark 9). When all the parcels are ready, bake them in the very hot oven for about 10 minutes or until the pastry is golden – keep an eye on them as they should not be overcooked. Serve with the Basil and Tomato Vinaigrette (see page 60) and a green salad.

BASIL AND TOMATO VINAIGRETTE
♣

This is a very useful (and delicious!) salad which can be served by itself as a starter (appetizer) or as one of several salads at lunchtime, which is what I usually do. Basil and tomato really are a magical combination.

SERVES 8

120 ml (4 fl oz/¹/₂ cup) extra virgin olive oil
60 ml (2 fl oz/¹/₄ cup) fresh lemon juice
1 onion, peeled and finely chopped
60 ml (4 tbsp/¹/₄ cup) fresh basil, chopped
salt and black pepper
8-12 really good ripe tomatoes
to garnish, sprigs of fresh basil

Place all the ingredients, except the tomatoes, in a blender and process. Alternatively, you can place them all in a large empty coffee jar, replace the lid and shake the jar well until the contents are mixed together. Slice the tomatoes evenly and arrange on a large serving platter. Pour on the dressing and leave to marinate for 1 hour or more before serving. Garnish with sprigs of fresh basil.

HAZELNUT, LEMON AND HERB PASTA
♣

This makes a superb side dish as part of a main course, whether it contains meat or not. You can use any shape of pasta, but I find that something small, such as shells or spirals, works best.

SERVES 4

45 ml (3 tbsp/1 cup) fresh parsley, finely chopped
15 ml (1 tbsp) chopped fresh lemon thyme
60 g (2 oz/¹/₂ cup) hazelnuts
15 ml (1 tbsp) lemon juice
grated zest of 1 lemon
60 ml (2 fl oz/¹/₄ cup) sunflower oil
salt and black pepper
700 g (1 ¹/₂ lb) fresh pasta
15 ml (1 tbsp) sunflower oil

Process or blend together all the ingredients except the pasta and the 15 ml (1 tbsp) of sunflower oil. Bring a large pan of salted water to the boil, add the oil and boil the pasta until it is *al dente*. Toss the pasta and the hazelnut dressing together and serve immediately.

——————— • ———————

Simple dishes are often the best, because they allow the flavour of each ingredient to shine through in a delicious way. Basil and Tomato Vinaigrette (top) is a classic salad, and deservedly so. The sweeter and fresher the tomatoes (try to use home-grown ones if possible) the better the salad will taste. The Hazelnut, Lemon and Herb Pasta (bottom) has a wonderfully fresh flavour and makes a lovely light lunch when served with a mixed salad and some fresh Italian bread.

POTATO SALAD WITH DILL

♣

This salad is always so popular that there are never any leftovers, which is a shame as I love it!

SERVES 8

240 ml (8 fl oz/1 cup) plain yoghurt or fromage frais
240 ml (8 fl oz/1 cup) good quality mayonnaise
30 ml (2 tbsp/¼ cup) chopped fresh dill
7.5 ml (½ tbsp) chopped fresh parsley
salt and black pepper
900 g (2 lb) tiny new potatoes
to garnish, chopped fresh parsley

Blend or process together the yoghurt, fromage frais, dill, parsley and salt and pepper to taste. Chill until needed. Clean the new potatoes well and boil for about 15 minutes or until tender. Drain, cool and mix with the mayonnaise mixture. Serve garnished with parsley.

GOATS' CHEESE WITH PEARS

♣

This salad is perfect for a light lunch.

SERVES 4

1 large or 2 small lettuces
180 ml (6 fl oz/¾ cup) peanut oil
50 ml (2 fl oz/¼ cup) red wine vinegar
10 ml (2 tsp) Dijon mustard
450 g (1 lb) goats' cheese
4 ripe pears

Wash the lettuce thoroughly and leave to dry, then either shred or tear the leaves into fairly small pieces. Mix together the peanut oil, vinegar and mustard and season with salt and pepper. Cut the goat's cheese into slices. Core and slice the pears.

Arrange lettuce leaves on one side of each plate, and the slices of cheese and pear on the other, then pour on some of the dressing.

CHOCOLATE AND VANILLA GATEAU
♣

This is more like a cooked chocolate mousse than a cake; it is very very rich but quite irresistible. If you have a chocoholic visiting you it could be difficult to get rid of them until all this cake has been eaten!

SERVES ABOUT 10

FOR THE GATEAU
—
250 g (9 oz) very good dessert (semi-sweet) chocolate

10 ml (2 tsp) instant coffee powder or granules

30 ml (2 tbsp) brandy

30 ml (2 tbsp) water

4 eggs

5 ml (1 tsp) vanilla essence (extract)

50 g (2 oz/¹/₄ cup) caster (superfine) sugar

10 ml (2 tsp) cornflour (cornstarch)

25 g (1 oz/4 tbsp) cocoa powder

FOR THE FILLING
—
100 g (4 oz) milk chocolate

150 ml (5 fl oz/²/₃cup) double (heavy) cream

to garnish, ground cinnamon

Grease a 900 g (2 lb/4 cups) loaf tin (bread pan) and line it with baking parchment or greaseproof paper. Pre-heat the oven to 180°C (350°F/ Gas Mark 4). To make the cake, break the chocolate into small pieces and place in a heatproof bowl over a pan of boiling water. Add the coffee, brandy and water and heat gently until the chocolate has melted completely. Remove the bowl from the pan of water and stir carefully until the mixture is smooth and cool.

Whisk the eggs, vanilla essence (extract), sugar and cornflour (cornstarch) until very thick and pale, then fold in the cocoa powder and the cooled chocolate mixture until it is all combined. Turn the mixture into the prepared loaf tin and bake for about 1 hour or until a skewer inserted into the middle of the cake comes out clean. Leave the cake in the tin for a few minutes, then turn out on to a wire rack,

carefully remove the lining paper and leave to cool.

To make the filling, break the milk chocolate into small pieces. Pour the cream into a small saucepan and bring to the boil. Immediately take off the heat and stir in the milk chocolate until it has completely melted. Return the mixture to the heat and bring to the boil briefly, then remove from the heat and leave to cool and thicken.

Slice the cake lengthwise at 2.5 cm (1 in) intervals and sandwich the layers together with the filling. Refrigerate for about 15 minutes. Dust the top of the cake with ground cinnamon and serve accompanied by a jug of cream into which you have stirred a few drops of vanilla essence.

GINGER CRANACHAN

Although the raspberry version of this pudding is a classic Scottish recipe, this ginger variation is a little bit different. It is always a great success.

SERVES 4

300 ml (¹/₂ pint/1¹/₄ cups) double (heavy) cream

100 g (4 oz) chopped stem ginger

30 ml (2 tbsp) toasted oatmeal

45 ml (3 tbsp) whisky

30 ml (2 tbsp) runny honey

15 ml (1 tbsp) syrup from the stem ginger

4 brandy snap baskets

Whip the cream until it forms peaks, then very carefully fold in all the other ingredients except the brandy snap baskets and chill well until needed. Serve in the brandy snap baskets, which are available from many supermarkets and delicatessens.

—————— · ——————

Previous pages: Choose the smallest new potatoes you can find for the Potato Salad with Dill (left). The Goats' Cheese with Pears could just as easily be a starter (appetizer), in which case you might want to reduce the quantities or increase the servings, or can be served as the cheese course in a leisurely evening meal.

*Two delicious desserts – Ginger Cranachan (left) and
Chocolate and Vanilla Gateau (right). To enhance the
vanilla flavour of the gateau you could keep a vanilla pod
in the sugar you use for desserts and use it instead of the
caster (superfine) sugar in this recipe.*

—————— • ——————

HOME-MADE GINGER CHOCOLATES

♣

Home-made chocolates are one of the most wonderful ways of ending a meal. They can be made a week in advance.

MAKES ABOUT 24

FOR THE CHOCOLATES
—
75 g (3 oz) plain (semi-sweet) chocolate

50 g (2 oz/¹/₄ cup) butter

30 ml (2 tbsp) ginger wine

30 ml (2 tbsp) stem ginger, very finely chopped

30 ml (2 tbsp) double (heavy) cream

FOR DIPPING
—
50 g (2 oz/²/₃ cup) cocoa powder

175 g (6 oz) plain (semi-sweet) chocolate

50 g (2 oz/¹/₄ cup) butter

to decorate, chopped stem ginger

To make the chocolates, break the 75 g (3 oz) chocolate into small pieces and place in a mixing bowl with the 50 g (2 oz/¹/₄ cup) butter. Place the bowl over a pan of hot water and stir until melted

These Home-made Ginger Chocolates are a real treat, whether you make them for yourself or intend to give them away as presents for family or friends.

and combined. Stir in the ginger wine and chopped stem ginger. Remove from the heat and stir in the cream. Allow to cool, then chill until firm.

To roll out the chocolates, place the cocoa powder in a shallow dish. Dip your hands in the cocoa powder and shape small teaspoonfuls of the mixture into balls. Chill again. Break the 175 g (6 oz) chocolate into small pieces and place in a bowl with the 50 g (2 oz/¹/₄ cup) butter. Melt over a pan of hot water, stirring gently. Remove from the heat. Dip each chocolate into this mixture and leave on silicon paper until set. Place a small piece of stem ginger on top of each chocolate before it sets completely.

FRESH FRUIT DIP

♣

This is a fun pudding that is ideal for a relaxed supper. For a more formal meal, you could serve each guest with an individual pot of the dip and a plate of the fruit.

SERVES 4

FOR THE DIP
—
180 ml (6 fl oz/³/₄ cup) double (heavy) cream

180 ml (6 fl oz/³/₄ cup) natural (plain) Greek yoghurt

30 ml (2 tbsp) fresh lemon balm (balm), finely chopped

15 ml (1 tbsp) fresh mint leaves, finely chopped

30 ml (2 tbsp) maple syrup

2.5 g (¹/₂ tsp) ground cinnamon

pinch of grated nutmeg

FOR THE FRUIT
—
a selection of fresh fruit, such as sliced peaches, whole cherries on their stalks (stems), apple and pear slices dipped in lemon juice, melon pieces, Cape gooseberries, orange segments, whole strawberries and so on

To make the dip, whip the cream lightly, then mix it thoroughly with the yoghurt, herbs, maple syrup and spices. Chill for a couple of hours before serving. Prepare the fresh fruit as near the time of serving as possible. Serve the dip in a pretty bowl surrounded by the fresh fruit.

BLACKBERRY AND ROSE GERANIUM DESSERT

♣

This is a very simple dessert that I discovered in America. The flavours are subtle but memorable.

SERVES 4

225 g (8 oz/3 cups) blackberries
6-8 rose geranium leaves
15-30 ml (1-2 tbsp) caster (superfine) sugar
double (heavy) cream to serve with the blackberries
to garnish, rose geranium flowers

Check through the blackberries for stalks (stems) or damaged fruit. Rinse the geranium leaves and crush them gently to release their scent. Arrange layers of the blackberries and geranium leaves in a decorative dish. Finish with a layer of blackberries and sprinkle them with the sugar. Cover the bowl and chill for about 6-8 hours.

Just before serving, take the dish out of the refrigerator and remove the geranium leaves. Serve each person with a dish of the blackberries garnished with a rose geranium flower. Serve the cream separately in a pretty jug.

*Both the Fresh Fruit Dip (left) and Blackberry
and Rose Geranium Dessert (right) are spectacular ways
of using up a glut of summer or autumn fruits.*

———— · ————

SPICY APPLE PIE
♣

This is a spicy version of my mother's almost legendary apple pie. The pastry is wonderful yet very simple to make.

SERVES 8-10

6 large Bramley apples

30 ml (2 tbsp) water

700 g (1½ lb/5¾ cups) self-raising (self-rising) flour

450 g (1 lb/2 cups) white vegetable fat (shortening)

very cold water

45 ml (3 tbsp) demerara or light brown sugar

10 ml (2 tsp) ground allspice or cinnamon

15 ml (1 tbsp) milk

1 egg yolk

Peel, core and slice the apples, then cook them gently in the 30 ml (2 tbsp) water for about 5-10 minutes. Leave to cool.

Grease a 30 cm (12 in) pie dish (a deep, oval baking dish with a rim). Make the pastry by rubbing (cutting) the fat into the flour until it resembles breadcrumbs, then add enough very cold water to form a soft dough. Divide the dough in half. Roll out the first half on a well-floured board until it is large enough to fit the pie dish. Lift up the pastry by folding it over the rolling pin and place it in the pie dish. Mould the pastry into the sides and trim off any excess with a sharp knife.

Pre-heat the oven to 200°C (400°F/Gas Mark 6). Drain the apples and carefully arrange in the pastry shell. Sprinkle over the sugar and allspice or cinnamon. Roll out the other half of the dough. Moisten the edges of the bottom layer of pastry with water, then place the second piece of pastry over the pie to make a lid. Press gently around the edges and trim off the excess. Mix together the milk and egg yolk in a bowl and brush the top of the pastry with it. Cut out pastry scraps into leaves or fruit, brush with the milk and egg glaze and use to decorate the top of the pie. Bake for 25-30 minutes or until the pastry is cooked and golden brown.

SESAME CRUNCH
♣

This easily made cake is delicious and can either be served at teatime or, if cut into very small squares, with your after-dinner coffee.

MAKES 8 LARGE PIECES

100 g (4 oz/½ cup) butter

30 ml (2 tbsp) golden (corn) syrup

25 g (1 oz/2 tbsp) caster (superfine) sugar

175 g (6 oz/3 cups) rolled oats (oatmeal)

30 ml (2 tbsp) sesame seeds

15 ml (1 tbsp) coconut flakes

Pre-heat the oven to 190°C (375°F/Gas Mark 5). In a saucepan, combine the butter and golden (corn) syrup and heat gently until they have melted. Take off the heat and add all the other ingredients. Stir well. Grease a shallow baking sheet and press the mixture into it, taking care to fill the corners. Bake in the oven for about 25-35 minutes or until golden brown. Leave to cool in the baking sheet for a few minutes before cutting into squares with a sharp knife. Leave in the baking sheet to cool completely, then remove the squares and store them in an airtight tin.

Opposite: *For traditional desserts, nothing can beat Spicy Apple Pie (right) and Sesame Crunch (left). To make the pastry extra short, chill the pastry for about 30 minutes after forming it into a soft dough, then chill the pie again before baking it in the oven.*

·

CAPPUCCINO BOMBE

♣

This is a recipe from my friend Melissa who helps me with some of the recipes on my courses. It is really scrummy and will probably become a real family favourite. The stronger the coffee you use, the better the bombe will taste.

150 ml (5 fl oz/²/₃ cup) extremely strong black coffee

175 g (6 oz/heaped ³/₄ cup) caster (superfine) sugar

5 ml (1 tsp) gelatine

3 egg whites

300 ml (¹/₂ pint/1 ¹/₄ cups) double (heavy) cream

225 g (8 oz) plain (semi-sweet) chocolate, grated

to garnish, ground cinnamon and pieces of fruit half-dipped in chocolate

Boil the coffee with the sugar and gelatine for 5 minutes. Whisk the egg whites until they are stiff, then fold in the coffee, sugar and gelatine mixture. Whip the cream until it forms soft peaks and fold into the egg and coffee mixture. Pour into a 900 ml (2 pint/5 cup) freezerproof bowl or bombe mould and freeze.

When the mixture is completely frozen, take it out of the freezer. Scoop out the middle of the ice cream and pour in the grated chocolate. Replace the ice cream to cover the chocolate and re-freeze.

To serve, dip the bowl in very hot water for a few seconds to loosen the ice cream, then turn it out on to an attractive serving plate. Decorate with fruit half-dipped in chocolate and sprinkle the entire bombe very lightly with ground cinnamon.

The Cappuccino Bombe is one of those marvellous recipes that are simple to make yet taste and look as though you have spent hours trying to get them exactly right!

·

70

You have to plan in advance if you want to make Cherry and Cinnamon Brandy for a special occasion, but it tastes so good you will be glad you made the effort.

CHERRY AND CINNAMON BRANDY
♣

This is a wonderfully alcoholic way to enjoy cherries and makes a good gift, if you can bear to give it away.

450 g (1 lb) Morello cherries
225 g (8 oz/heaped 1 cup) caster (superfine) sugar
600 ml (1 pint/2 ¹/₂ cups) cheap brandy
12 blanched almonds
2 sticks cinnamon

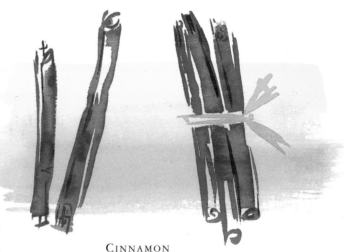

CINNAMON

Place alternate layers of clean dry cherries and caster (superfine) sugar in a dry Kilner jar. Fasten the top and leave in a cool place for 3 days, shaking the jar every now and then. Undo the lid and add the brandy, almonds and cinnamon sticks. Fasten the lid again tightly and leave for at least 3 months. When ready to use, strain the liquid carefully and pour it into a clean bottle.

GINGER BEER
♣

This is a lovely old-fashioned drink. I know you can buy it in the shops but it's fun to make your own sometimes.

MAKES 4.8 LITRES (8 PINTS/5 QUARTS)

4.8 litres (8 pints/5 quarts) water
175 g (6 oz/5$^{1}/_{3}$ tbsp) root ginger
50 g (2 oz/5$^{1}/_{3}$ tbsp) cream of tartar
900 g (2 lb/4$^{1}/_{2}$ tbsp) white sugar
grated zest and juice of 3 lemons
30 ml (2 tbsp) fresh yeast

Boil the water. Bruise the ginger, then cut it into 2.5-cm (1-in) thick slices and place it in a very large bowl with the cream of tartar, sugar and lemon zest and pour on the water. Stir vigorously until the sugar has dissolved, then leave to cool. Add the yeast and lemon juice, cover with a thick cloth and leave to stand for 24 hours in a warm room. After this time, remove the scum that will have formed and pour off the liquid, trying not to disturb the sediment at the bottom, and bottle as soon as possible. The ginger beer will be ready to drink in 2-3 days.

CIDER TODDY
♣

You can try this to help stave off a cold or to make yourself feel better if you already have one. That may or may not be an old wives' tale but the toddy certainly tastes good!

7.5 g ($^{1}/_{4}$ oz) root ginger
1 glass cider (hard cider)
twist lemon peel
10 ml (2 tsp) honey

Bruise the root ginger with a rolling pin, then heat it with the cider and lemon peel in a small pan until the liquid begins to bubble. Take off the heat, stir in the honey and strain the liquid into a warmed glass or mug.

RHUBARB CORDIAL
♣

If you enjoy the flavour of rhubarb you will love this unusual drink which is especially refreshing on a hot summer's day.

7.5 g ($^{1}/_{4}$ oz) root ginger
900 g (2 lb/7$^{1}/_{4}$ cups) rhubarb, chopped
100 g (4 oz/$^{1}/_{2}$ cup) caster (superfine) sugar
2 cloves
1.2 litres (2 pints/5 cups) water
to garnish, mint leaves

Bruise the root ginger with a rolling pin. Place the rhubarb, sugar, cloves and ginger in a large saucepan and pour in the water. Bring to the boil and simmer gently until the rhubarb is soft, replacing any water that evaporates. Strain well and pour into a warmed glass jug. Garnish with a few mint leaves.

———— • ————

Opposite: In the days before it was easy to buy ready-made drinks from the shops, people would make their own soft drinks and cordials. You can revive that tradition by making Cider Toddy (top), Rhubarb Cordial (left) or Ginger Beer (right).

CUCUMBER AND MINT RAITA

This raita is also good as a salad dressing or a dip.

1/2 cucumber
15 ml (1 tbsp) finely chopped fresh mint
15 ml (1 tbsp) finely chopped fresh dill
240 ml (8 fl oz/1 cup) thick Greek yoghurt
30 ml (2 tbsp) lemon juice
15 ml (1 tbsp) olive oil
salt and black pepper

Peel the cucumber and slice it in half lengthways. Scoop out the pips (seeds) and discard. Cut the cucumber into slices and place in a colander. Sprinkle with salt and leave to drain for about 1 hour. Rinse with cold water and dry, then chop very finely or grate. Mix together the herbs, yoghurt, lemon juice and olive oil and mix well. Stir in the cucumber, season to taste and chill for 1 hour before serving.

BANANA RAITA

This is another raita that is great with curries. However, as not everyone likes coconut I usually serve both raitas.

15 g (1/2 oz/1 tbsp) butter
5 ml (1 tsp) coriander seeds
30 ml (2 tbsp) coconut flakes
salt and black pepper
2 small bananas, peeled
240 ml (8 fl oz/1 cup) thick Greek yoghurt

Melt the butter in a saucepan and sauté the coriander seeds and coconut flakes with plenty of freshly ground black pepper until golden brown. Finely chop the bananas and mix with the coconut mixture and the yoghurt. Season to taste and chill for 1 hour before serving.

———————— · ————————

Opposite: *Two cooling side dishes to accompany curries – Cucumber and Mint Raita (back) and Banana Raita (front).*

CHEESE AND HERB LOAF

♣

This recipe can be adapted endlessly according to the fresh herbs or flour that you have available.

240 ml (8 fl oz/1 cup) lukewarm milk

15 ml (1 tbsp) sugar

1 medium egg, beaten

10 ml (2 tsp) dried yeast

15 ml (1 tbsp) fresh dill, chopped

15 ml (1 tbsp) fresh tarragon, chopped

30 ml (2 tbsp/¼ cup) spring onions (scallions), chopped

5 ml (1 tsp) salt

5 ml (1 tsp) black pepper

30 ml (2 tbsp) sunflower oil

225 g (8 oz/1¾ cups) wholemeal (whole-wheat) flour

450 g (1 lb/2 cups) strong (hard) white flour, sifted

100 g (4 oz/1 cup) Cheddar cheese, grated

to garnish, poppy seeds

In a large bowl, mix together the milk, sugar, beaten egg, dried yeast, herbs and spring onions (scallions) with the salt and pepper. Stir in 15 ml (1 tbsp) sunflower oil. Stir in the flours, a little at a time, until the dough is stiff enough to knead – if necessary, add a little more white flour to stiffen the dough.

Turn the dough on to a clean floured board and knead in the grated Cheddar cheese. Knead the dough well for about 10 minutes. Lightly oil a clean mixing bowl and place the dough in it, brushing the top with a little oil. Cover with a clean damp tea towel and leave in a warm place for about 1 hour or until it has doubled in size. Knock back to deflate the dough and turn it out again on to the floured board. Knead it again for a couple of minutes, then place in an oiled 1.2 litre (2 pint/5 cups) loaf tin (bread pan) and leave to rise for another hour. Pre-heat the oven to 190°C (375°F/Gas Mark 5). Brush the top of the loaf with the remaining 15 ml (1 tbsp) of sunflower oil and cover with the poppy seeds. Bake for about 45-50 minutes or until the crust is golden brown and the loaf sounds hollow when you tap its base. Allow to cool on a wire cooling rack.

When making the Cheese and Herb Loaf you can alter the proportions of wholemeal (whole-wheat) to white flour, or add small amounts of other flours, such as rye.

SAGE, ONION AND THYME RELISH

♣

This relish is wonderful with traditional or home-made pork sausages and turns them into a family favourite.

2 very large onions, peeled

2 leeks

50 g (2 oz/¼ cup) butter

15 ml (1 tbsp) red wine vinegar

150 ml (¼ pint/⅔ cup) good red wine

30 ml (2 tbsp) demerara or light brown sugar

5 ml (1 tsp) fresh thyme, chopped

5 ml (1 tsp) fresh sage leaves, chopped

salt and freshly ground black pepper

Chop the onions and leeks. Melt the butter in a saucepan and sauté the onions and leeks, stirring frequently, until soft. Add the vinegar, wine and sugar and simmer for 20 minutes until most of the liquid has evaporated. Add the thyme and sage, and season to taste. Pour into hot clean jam jars and seal tightly. Label when cool.

GOOSEBERRY AND LEMON JELLY

♣

Herb and fruit jellies are an invaluable addition to everyday meals – they can liven up the most mundane pork steak or lamb chop. This jelly is also delicious on scones at teatime.

900 g (2 lb) eating apples

900 g (2 lb) gooseberries

30 ml (2 tbsp) lemon juice

5 ml (1 tsp) grated lemon zest

750 ml (1¼ pints/3 cups) water

30 ml (2 tbsp) fresh lemon balm (balm), chopped

15 ml (1 tbsp) fresh lemon thyme, chopped

700 g (1½ lb/3½ cups) preserving sugar

Wash, core and chop the apples, but leave on their skins. Place the apples, gooseberries, lemon juice and zest in a large saucepan, add the water and 15 ml (1 tbsp) lemon balm. Bring to the boil and simmer, covered, for about 30 minutes or until the fruit is soft. Remove from the heat and strain through a fine cloth or jelly strainer into a large clean bowl. Discard the pulp. Measure the liquid produced – add a cup of sugar to each cup of liquid and place in a clean large saucepan. Bring to the boil and boil rapidly for about 15 minutes or until the jelly reaches setting point. If you are using a sugar (candy) thermometer, setting point is at 105°C (221°F). Alternatively, spoon a little jelly on to a chilled saucer, allow to cool and then push your finger across its surface – the jelly will wrinkle when it has reached setting point. Leave to stand for about 5 minutes, then add the lemon thyme and the rest of the lemon balm and stir well. Pour into hot, clean jam jars and seal tightly. Label when cool.

Both the Sage, Onion and Thyme Relish (left) and the Gooseberry and Lemon Jelly (right) are easy to prepare and are good additions to your store cupboard (pantry).

FENNEL, PARSLEY AND ALMOND CHEESE SPREAD
♣

Thinking up new and inspiring sandwich fillings is difficult if you have to provide packed lunches every day.

75 g (3 oz/³/4 cup) mature Cheddar cheese, grated
25 g (1 oz/2 tbsp) Feta cheese, crumbled
50 g (2 oz/¹/4 cup) ricotta cheese
15 ml (1 tbsp) fresh parsley, chopped
30 ml (2 tbsp) fennel leaves, chopped
30 ml (2 tbsp) blanched almonds, chopped
salt and black pepper

Place all the cheeses in a food processor and combine well. Add the remaining ingredients and process again until thoroughly blended. Season to taste. Chill in the refrigerator until required.

Fresh herbs really come into their own with Dill Pesto (left), which is a variation of the classic Italian sauce, and Fennel, Parsley and Almond Cheese Spread (right).

DILL PESTO
♣

This is quite delicious when served on a baked potato or mixed with the dressing on a potato salad. You can also mix it with mayonnaise and serve it with salmon.

1 small clove of garlic, peeled
1 large handful fresh dill
2 sprigs fresh parsley
small handful fresh chives
45 ml (3 tbsp) matured Cheddar cheese, grated
45 ml (3 tbsp) walnuts, pecan or pistachio nuts
salt and black pepper
60 ml (4 tbsp) olive oil

Place the garlic, dill, parsley and chives in a food processor and process until finely chopped. Add the cheese, nuts and salt and black pepper and process again. Slowly add the oil while the processor is running until combined. Store in the refrigerator.

AVOCADO AND HERB DIP
♣

You can serve this dip either as a dip or as a starter (appetizer), with pitta bread or tortilla chips. If serving it as a starter, place a small amount on each plate.

1 handful coriander leaves (cilantro)
1 handful parsley leaves
1 clove garlic, peeled
30 ml (2 tbsp) lime juice
salt and black pepper
60 ml (4 tbsp/¹/4 cup) sunflower oil
15 ml (1 tbsp) lemon juice
3 small avocados

Place the herbs and garlic in a food processor and process until finely chopped. Add the lime juice, salt and pepper and process again. Slowly add the oil, while the processor is running. Cut the avocados in half, remove the stones (pits) and scoop out the flesh into the food processor. Add the lemon juice, then process again until thoroughly mixed.

78

Two refreshing and unusual ways with herbs – Avocado and Herb Dip (top) includes coriander leaves (cilantro) and Herby Mayonnaise (bottom) has dill, basil and tarragon.

————— • —————

HERBY MAYONNAISE
♣

Following the recent scares about the possible presence of salmonella in some raw eggs, I have stopped making my own mayonnaise and use a good commercial brand instead.

600 ml (1 pint/2 1/2 cups) mayonnaise
15 ml (1 tbsp) fresh parsley
15 ml (1 tbsp) fresh dill
15 ml (1 tbsp) fresh basil
15 ml (1 tbsp) fresh chives
15 ml (1 tbsp) fresh tarragon

Place all the herbs in a food processor and process until finely chopped. Add the mayonnaise and process again until well combined. Alternatively, you can chop the herbs by hand and mix them with the mayonnaise in a bowl with a wooden spoon.

You can substitute other herbs for the ones I have mentioned here, just use one variety on its own or add some crushed garlic.

HERBAL AND SPICED VINEGARS
♣

Herbal and/or spiced vinegars are very simple to make and add an extra dimension to your cooking. Most vinegars (except for malt vinegar) are suitable, but I generally use a good cider or wine vinegar.

whole spices and fresh herbs of your choice
vinegar of your choice

Wash and dry the fresh herbs and place them, with the spices, in a clean glass bottle that has either a screw-top lid or a cork. Fill up with vinegar, seal tightly and label. Leave on a sunny windowsill for at least a week before using.

Among the many combinations that work well are marjoram, chives and whole peppercorns with red wine vinegar; chervil, tarragon and whole cloves of garlic with white wine vinegar; basil, onion slices and peppercorns with cider vinegar.

Herbal and Spiced Vinegars give a real lift to marinades, salad dressings, mayonnaise and many other dishes. They also look very attractive on the kitchen windowsill.

————— • —————

HERBAL AND SPICED OILS

♣

*As with the vinegars, herbal and spiced oils are extremely
simple to make and delicious to eat. It is best to produce them
in relatively small amounts, as these oils have a very intense
flavour. I use sunflower oil as any stronger oil could not
compete against the flavours of the herbs and spices.*

whole spices and fresh herbs of your choice
sunflower oil

Wash and dry the fresh herbs and place them,
with the spices, in a clean glass bottle that has
either a screw-top lid or a cork. Fill up with oil, seal
tightly and label. Leave on a sunny windowsill for at
least a week before using.

Among the many combinations that work well are
chilli (chili pepper), garlic and whole black
peppercorns; sage, thyme and onion; rosemary and
whole black peppercorns; basil and garlic; dill, chives
and red onion slices.

*Make Herbal and Spiced Oils in the summer months when
you have plenty of fresh herbs to spare, ready to brighten up
your cooking during the autumn and winter. They also
make good presents for keen cooks.*

———— • ————

DECORATING
WITH
HERBS AND SPICES

On the following pages you will find all

sorts of ideas and instructions for decorating

your home with herbs and spices. The sections

are organized room by room, so your whole

house can smell fragrant and look decorative.

ENTRANCE HALL

♣

The entrance to your house is a very important area as it provides the first impression that guests will have of you and your way of life. A very grand entrance will no doubt impress people but a warm welcoming atmosphere will give an even better impression as your friends arrive. Whether you are greeting people you have invited round for a special occasion or just a friend who's popped in on the off-chance, it's good to know there's an attractive arrangement or feature in the entrance hall, on the front door or even going up the stairs, which will provide an interesting talking point and a warm welcome. Having said that, many of our friends automatically come to the back door which leads straight into the dog's room – not that she isn't an attractive feature! – and usually past buckets of flowers and other useful paraphernalia that is waiting to be made into something!

This section of the book is full of ideas for making arrangements using herbs and spices, but don't forget the simple effectiveness of a vase of fresh flowers.

――――――― · ―――――――

DRIED PEONY AND HERB WREATH

A welcome wreath on your front door looks very attractive and can be made from fresh or dried flowers or herbs. The ring of peonies and herbs pictured here was made from dried ingredients, so would not be suitable for outdoor use in a damp climate. Dried flowers do not react well to low temperatures, dampness or humidity so it is best to display this sort of arrangement indoors. You could hang it on the back of the door, on a wall in the hall, or you may have a porch that would keep the damp and cold away from the flowers.

To make it, you will need any ready-made twiggy wreath as a base, a hot glue gun (other types of glue may not be strong enough to hold everything in place), some small lightweight baskets, some dark green reindeer moss, light green hydrangea heads, pink ('Sarah Bernhardt') peonies, bunches of various dried herbs and pale pink helichrysum (straw flower) heads.

Cut the baskets in half, to make them easier to glue on to the wreath, then glue them into position with the hot glue gun while they are empty. When you glue on the baskets, remember that they should all be pointing upwards, or at least at an angle at which the contents could stay in place without defying gravity – it looks rather odd to have baskets hanging upside down while the ingredients happily stay in position! Between the baskets, glue on clumps of the dark green reindeer moss and the light green hydrangea heads.

The pink 'Sarah Bernhardt' peonies should be attached next. Gently ease open the flowers as much as possible, without damaging them or making the petals fall out, then glue them on to the wreath. I glued them in clumps of three or more to give a stronger effect. Now make up some small bunches of various herbs (I used a mixture of marjoram, oregano and lavender) and glue them into the baskets so they spill out in a convincing way. Finally, add a few pale pink helichrysum heads to fill any odd gaps left in the design – there always seem to be some.

*This Dried Peony and Herb Wreath can be hung up
indoors or out, according to the general climate, because
dried flowers go floppy in damp atmospheres.*

BANISTER GARLAND

Another area that looks spectacular if it is decorated is the staircase. I realize that flowers on the banisters, or anything large and fragile near the stairs, can be a tremendous nuisance for everyday use but on special occasions decorations like this can look wonderful. I think garlands look spectacular when twisted around the banister rail, although it is not a suitable decoration if you have very young children or very old or infirm people in the house as they may need to hold on to the banister rail to keep their balance as they go up and down stairs.

The base of this garland is a rope of paper ribbon, the kind that you buy twisted up, ready to unravel for use as bows and for decorating arrangements. However, in this case you want to leave it in its original twisted state as a rope, so you can wire all the ingredients on to it. To make it, you will need the paper rope, and plenty of air-dried eucalyptus leaves, grouped into small bunches of two or three sprays each, about 10 cm (4 in) long and wired together. You will also need some dried *Limonium latifolium* (statice) which has been tinted with dye to give it a strong lavender colour, and some cream xeranthemum daisies, also wired into small bunches. In addition, you will need some pine cones which have been scented with suitable herbal essential oils to add a subtle aroma to the garland. Wire up each cone by tightly wrapping a heavy-gauge wire around the base of the scales, twist it together and leave a long leg with which to wire the cone into the garland. You will also need some liquorice (licorice) root, which is the star of the garland. These long straight sticks should be bundled together, nine at a time, and tied with medium-gauge wire. Cover the wire with raffia which has been firmly tied in a single knot. Finally, you will need some ribbons to decorate the garland.

Measure the length of paper ribbon that you will need, allowing for it to twist around the banister, and add at least 5 cm (2 in) at each end for loops. Bend each of these spare sections of rope over on itself and tightly bind a length (piece) of heavy-gauge wire around it to form a secure loop, so you can hang up the garland. Then, using medium-gauge wire, start to attach the eucalyptus, statice, daisies and pine cones evenly on to the paper rope. Start at one end and work towards the middle, then turn the garland round and repeat the process from the other end. When you have reached the centre and have the ends of the eucalyptus stems touching, fill in the gap by wiring in some individual eucalyptus stems at right angles to the rope until the middle is filled with foliage.

Now attach the ribbons. For this garland I used a wide ribbon that is wired down both sides, as this gives you more flexibility and means you can put the ribbon wherever you want it, in the knowledge that it will stay in place. However, its drawback is its price, and you could easily use a less expensive ribbon. Wire the ribbon into loops, and then either wire them on the garland with more wire or attach them with your trusty glue gun. The ribbons can be placed wherever you like on the garland, but it is a good idea to start in the centre as they will cover up any less-than-perfect wiring that might be there! I also put ribbons at each end but this is not necessary, just a matter of personal choice.

Finally, place your garland full length on the table or surface on which you are working and assess where the bundles of liquorice root should go. If they are placed too close together they will make the garland look too heavy in some places and too light in others, so arrange them with care.

It is a good idea, when you think you've finished, to leave the garland where it is and do something else for a while. When you come back to it you will probably see it with fresh eyes and be able to spot any gaps or unsightly areas that you missed before. Incidentally, do make sure you have wired in all the ends of the wires, and not left them sticking out, otherwise they might easily catch in someone's clothes or tear their skin. When you are satisfied, you are ready to hang the garland in place, although you might need some help if you don't want it to drag on the ground and undo all your hard work.

––––––––– · –––––––––

Here are two decorations suitable for an entrance hall – the Banister Garland, with its bundles of liquorice (licorice) root, and the Hall Table Arrangement.

HALL TABLE ARRANGEMENT

Flower arrangements in halls look wonderful, and a good place to put one would be on a small hall table or letter stand. Many entrance halls are fairly dark so are the ideal places for dried arrangements, as the lack of light will prolong the life of the flowers and prevent them fading too quickly. This arrangement was designed to tie in with the wreath on the front door, so I used the main ingredients again.

You will need a medium to large open basket, dried flower foam, either some dried hydrangea heads or plenty of *Limonium dumosa* (statice or sea lavender), bunches of dried pink and pale blue larkspur, bunches of dried medium-sized poppy seed heads, about seven dried pink 'Sarah Bernhardt' peonies, small wired bunches of various dried herbs and some ribbons.

Fill the basket with blocks of the dried flower foam, then camouflage this with the hydrangea heads or statice, depending on what you have chosen. You will need more sea lavender than hydrangea heads, because it is much smaller. Now arrange bunches of

This Hall Table Arrangement, in shades of pinks and blues, is crammed with dried peonies, lavender, larkspur, poppy seed heads and a selection of dried herbs.

the pink larkspur throughout the basket, making sure you keep an evenly round shape to the arrangement and that it is slightly taller than the statice. Put in some bunches of pale blue larkspur next, making sure they are the same height as the pink variety. Next, add the bunches of poppy seed heads, but first cut their stems so they are slightly shorter than the larkspur but longer than the statice. Their lovely grey colour goes very well with the other colours in this arrangement and their interesting shapes add important texture. Cut the stems of the peonies so they are the same length as the poppy seed heads, otherwise their size and shape will overpower everything else in the basket. Add them to the arrangement so they are evenly spread throughout the basket. Finally, fill in the gaps with small wired bunches of the herbs – I used marjoram, lavender and oregano. The look of these herbs is much improved by grouping them in small clumpy bunches because they are too wispy and inconspicuous when used as individual stems. The stems should be cut to no more than 7.5 cm (3 in) and each bundle should not be any thicker than your little finger. It does not matter if the ends of the stems don't reach into the foam as they can be pushed in against all the other stems and will happily stay in position like that. Finally, add the ribbons – I used a navy paisley design that blended in with the lavender, blue and pink tones.

DECORATED POT POURRI BASKET

If you want to have some flowers in the hall but would also like the scent of pot pourri, you could make a decorated basket to fill with pot pourri. This shallow basket has flowers decorating the base of both ends of the handle but, as it is so attractive, I have left the rest of it undecorated. To make a similar basket to the one shown in the photograph, you will need a shallow basket, some tiny 3.5-cm (1½-in) terracotta flowerpots, bunches of dried marjoram, cream peonies, pale yellow roses, small wired bunches of glycerined gypsophila (baby's breath) – place the stems in a jug of equal quantities of glycerine and water and leave until the flowers have turned an attractive cream colour – and some ribbon.

*Filling a wide and shallow basket like this with
pot pourri will help to scent your hallway and provide
a fragrant welcome for guests.*

•

The ribbon I chose was a dark mauve flowered design, and first I wired it into fairly large loops, then glued them into place around the base of each handle. Fill the tiny flowerpots with the bunches of marjoram and fix them in position with dabs from the hot glue gun. Alternatively, you can fill the pots with dried flower foam and push the marjoram stalks (stems) into it, but that can be very fiddly and it is much quicker to work with the glue gun. The rest of the design is equally quick to make because it is all glued in place. Attach the flowerpots in a cluster around each handle, ensuring the marjoram points at different angles but never upside down. Fill the space between the pots with the cream peonies and pale yellow roses, holding them in place with dabs of glue. Finally, to give a dainty touch, add some small sprigs of the glycerined gypsophila. Don't make these too

I like to collect old jugs and other interesting containers because they are invaluable vases for flowers, whether fresh, as shown in this photograph, or dried.

large or long, or they will look too leggy and spoil the shape of your arrangement.

The pot pourri inside this basket was designed after I had made the basket, as I wanted it to tone in with the colours of the ribbon and the flowers. Obviously you could buy some ready-made pot pourri that looks suitable or just use some pine cones scented with a suitable essential oil, but making your own pot pourri is great fun, very simple and quickly becomes addictive. It is an especially satisfying pastime if you have also grown all the floral and leafy ingredients and dried them yourself.

1 handful dried hydrangea florets
1 handful dried hibiscus seed heads
1 handful dried marjoram florets
1 handful small pine cones
1 handful bougainvillaea petals
12 ml (2 heaped tsp) powdered orris root
15 ml (1 tbsp) essential or perfume oils of your choice

Place all the dry ingredients, except the pine cones, in a large ceramic or glass mixing bowl and stir thoroughly with a metal spoon (a wooden one will absorb all the oil). Decide whether the quantity will be enough to fill the basket you have in mind, or whether you should use more ingredients. Alternatively, you can add padding to a deep basket by filling the base with crumpled tissue paper, or something similar, to reduce the amount of pot pourri you will need. Ensure the powdered orris root is well mixed in with the other ingredients, then drop in the oil or oils (I used equal amounts of ginger, orange and cinnamon essential oils) and stir again thoroughly. When everything has been mixed together well, add the pine cones and stir again. It is important to add the pine cones after the oil becausel, if you do it the other way round, they seem to soak up all the oil and everything else stays unscented.

Tip the mixture into a large plastic bag and tie up the neck tightly. Leave the mixture to mature for a week or so in a warm airy place, shaking it whenever you remember. When it is ready, tip it into the decorated basket and display it in the hall.

COUNTRY KITCHEN

♣

For me, the kitchen is the heart of any home and our kitchen is probably my favourite room in the whole house. We have long since turned our dining room into an office and, because our kitchen is very large, we prefer to have a big table in there where our friends and family gather, whether I want them to watch me cooking or not! Obviously this fits in well with our relaxed country life, in which mud appears from nowhere and spreads everywhere; if it's not the dog leaving muddy footprints then it's a daughter!

Of course it may be a different story for you if you have a lovely elegant home in a city, and your entertaining could well be very different. A beautiful dining room is a great asset, but you can still make your kitchen an enjoyable place in which to work.

KITCHEN WREATH

This ring looks wonderful when it is finally finished, but I certainly couldn't recommend it as a quickie to throw together just before your guests arrive! However, to look on the bright side, the bonus with this wreath (as with all dried flower arrangements) is that after hours of hard work you can admire your craftsmanship for months or even years to come whereas, on a bad day, a fresh arrangement will wilt before your very eyes. The best way to tackle a design like this is to make it over several days, so you contribute something to it each day rather than sit at it for hours on end until you lose patience with it.

To make it, you will need a large twiggy wreath, two lengths (pieces) of twisted paper rope in toning

Kitchens often have large windows which let in plenty
of light, so a very simple decoration for them would be
a container planted with a few spring bulbs.

colours to match your kitchen, tissue paper, various dried pulses, quails' eggs, large pieces of root ginger, a large tapestry (needlepoint) needle, thin wool (yarn) to match the paper rope, a hot glue gun and a selection of small dried flowers.

Cut off enough of one of the paper ropes to make a lavish bow, then untwist the rope, tie it into the bow (which should be large without being so huge that it overpowers all the other ingredients) and place on one side. Untwist more of each rope and cut it into pieces about 20 cm (8 in) long. Fold these pieces in half and sew up the two sides with the wool, using blanket stitch, to create tiny sacks in the two colours. When you have finished making the sacks (I used twelve for my wreath) you should stuff each one with crumpled tissue paper to pad it out, then place the dried pulses on top. If you fill the entire sack with beans it will be too heavy for the glue to hold it firmly on the wreath. To fix the beans inside each sack, I squirted a layer of glue on the tissue paper first, poured in the beans and left the glue to dry, then repeated the operation with more layers of glue and beans until the sack was full. Finally, to get the effect of the beans spilling out of each sack, you must use a pair of tweezers to glue each bean in place. Be warned – this is an irritating but necessary process. It was tolerable with the red

It can take time to make a wreath, especially if you have never done it before, so don't be in too much of a hurry or you might make mistakes.

kidney beans because they are quite large, but the green lentils began to annoy me and once I had reached the small orange split lentils I was wondering why on earth I'd had this bright idea in the first place! So you might like to modify your choice of ingredients and use pasta, coffee beans or nuts instead of the lentils.

You must blow the quails' eggs before adding them to the arrangement. Always buy more eggs than you think you will need to allow for breakages. To blow the eggs, leave them at room temperature for at least an hour, then carefully make a hole in both ends of each egg with a large tapestry needle. Push the needle into the egg and gently wiggle it around to break the yolk and mix it with the white, then blow gently through one end while holding the egg over a bowl to catch the contents. When the egg is empty, rinse it and leave it to drain.

Another preparatory task is to make small bunches of the various floral ingredients you want to use. For this wreath I chose pale blue larkspur, a little broom bloom sprayed the same blue colour as the larkspur, some green *Limonium dumosa* (Statice or sea lavender), dried poppy seed heads and green wheat ears. Make several small bunches about 7.5-10 cm (3-4 in) long of each type of flower and wire them firmly around the base – this will save a lot of time when it comes to making up the wreath.

You have now reached the point where you can assemble the wreath. First fix on the bow, using the hot glue gun. Then carefully attach the sacks of ingredients, again using the hot glue gun. If you are using a variety of pulses, as I did, make sure they are evenly spaced around the wreath and you don't have all the orange lentils on one side and all the green on the other. When all the sacks are firmly in position, start glueing on the small bunches of dried flowers and wheat. I put the wheat on first as it is very long and therefore quite difficult to position easily.

Gradually build up the wreath all the way round until it is bursting with flowers and the other ingredients. When you are happy with the way it looks, add the finishing touches of the large pieces of root ginger and clumps of the quails' eggs.

*I made this wreath for the kitchen from objects you
would expect to find in most kitchens, such as eggs and
various pulses, as well as pieces of root ginger.*

———————— • ————————

DECORATED BREAD BOARD

When you are decorating your kitchen with herbs, spices or flowers it is nice to choose objects that stay within the theme of the kitchen, rather than things that belong to different rooms in the house. For instance, this decorated bread board is perfect for a casual wall decoration, or even as a table centre, and is quick and easy to make. If you want to hang the finished bread board on the wall, you should attach some appropriate hooks, bought from a picture framer's, to the back of the board before you start work (it will be extremely difficult to do it once the arrangement is finished). Alternatively, you can buy a bread board that already has a handle with a hole bored in it.

To make this decoration, you will need some dried-out bread rolls, dried apple slices, small decorative objects (I chose a tiny terracotta jug and some miniature wicker wreaths that I stained a darker colour), unshelled walnuts, dried flowers (I used *Achillea filipendula* or fernleaf yellow yarrow), some salignum cones and some herbs (for this design, I used dried marjoram and rosemary picked straight from the garden so it could dry out in the arrangement). You will also need a hot glue gun.

Before you start assembling the bread board you need to do some preliminary work. Buy the smallest bread rolls you can find (or make your own, if you have the time) and place them on a baking sheet in a low oven (about 150°C/300°F/Gas Mark 2) for several hours until they feel very light but are rock hard when you tap them. Leave them to cool, then spray with matt polyurethane varnish all over to prevent insects or other creatures (such as dogs!) deciding to make a snack out of them.

Another piece of preparation you can do in advance is prepare the apple slices, which can then be dried out in the oven at the same time as the bread rolls. Choose a couple of red-skinned apples that are in good condition – it is no good using up old bruised or wrinkled specimens for this as they will just look second-rate when they have dried. Stand the apples on a board, with the stalks (stems) pointing upwards, and cut them into thin even slices. Place these slices on a baking sheet and brush them on both sides with lemon juice – this will ensure they stay a pale colour and do not turn an unattractive brown. Then place in a low oven with the bread rolls and leave for at least 40 minutes. Keep an eye on them every now and then as the exact length of time they need depends on the thickness of the slices and the variety of apple. They are dry when they feel like leather. Take them out of the oven and leave to cool.

When you have assembled all the ingredients you can begin attaching them to the board with the hot glue gun. Start with the rolls, as they need to be firmly attached to the wood, then add the jugs and wreaths, or any similar decorations you are using. Then add the rosemary, achillea, marjoram and walnuts and, finally, tuck in the apple slices.

DECORATED ROLLING PIN

When you have successfully produced the bread board, how about making a matching rolling pin to hang near it? It will look most effective if you use the same ingredients as the ones for the bread board, plus some dried chillies (chili peppers) which are easily bought from health food stores and delicatessens.

Choose a long piece of ribbon in a toning colour and firmly tie one end to each end of the rolling pin so it acts as a hanging loop. Again, you should attach the bread rolls first, bearing in mind the angle from which the rolling pin will be viewed. Then glue on the rosemary and achillea, making sure you also hide the place where the ribbon is knotted on each handle. Add some apple slices and a few chillies, which should be glued on individually. As a finishing touch, make a pretty bow with long streamers, using the same ribbon as before, and glue it on to the centre of the ribbon, to disguise the hook it will hang from. For the sake of accuracy it is best to hang up the finished rolling pin before you do this, otherwise it's all too easy to get the bow off-centre.

·———·

If you don't already have a hot glue gun, I would heartily recommend you buy one, otherwise glueing objects to the bread board and rolling pin could be very difficult.

SPICY GARLAND

Lots of kitchens need brightening up, and a garland of dried flowers is the perfect solution. Just make sure it isn't in a very steamy part of the kitchen otherwise the dried flowers will become damp and floppy.

The base of this kitchen garland is a rope of twisted paper ribbon – the same as I used for the garland around the banisters (see page 86). The ingredients were bunches of glycerined beech leaves, bay leaves wired into bunches of three and five, bunches of five chillies (chili peppers), bunches of three pieces of root ginger, bundles of cinnamon sticks and some blown quails' eggs (see page 92). You should also prepare bunches of wheat, marjoram and oregano, making all of them roughly the same size. You will also need some medium-gauge wire, a hot glue gun and some ribbon in a toning colour.

Measure the length of garland that you will need and add about 5 cm (2 in) to each end for the loops. To make each one, bend the 5 cm (2 in) back on itself and wire it firmly to make a loop. Then, using a medium-gauge wire, attach a bunch of beech leaves at one end of the garland and wire in the other ingredients as you progress towards the middle. Do not add the ginger, chillies, cinnamon and quails' eggs at this stage. Once you have reached the middle of the garland, turn it round and start from the other end with another bunch of beech leaves. When you reach the middle and have wired in as many ingredients as possible there will be a gap, so take some slightly shorter sprigs of beech leaves and wire them in at right angles to the ribbon to fill the gap.

When you are happy with the way the garland looks, make some ribbon loops (I used a dark purple wired ribbon), wire them into shape and glue them into the garland. Then attach the ginger, chillies, cinnamon and quails' eggs, using the hot glue gun. Lay the garland out flat and have a critical look at it. If there are any noticeable gaps I would suggest you

As the Spicy Garland is heavy you will have to use several nails when hanging it up – one at each end for the loops and perhaps a couple in the middle for added support.

cheat slightly and glue in a bunch or two of flowers or leaves to cover the space. You will also need to check whether the garland has an equal width and weight along its entire length – again, fill in any thin areas using the hot glue gun.

FLAT-BACKED BREAD BASKET

The final idea for the kitchen is a flat-backed basket to hang on the wall. Most of these ideas have been designed to hang on the wall because work surfaces are usually at a premium in the kitchen – also it is probably slightly more hygienic to have dried flowers (in other words, dust traps) hanging on the walls rather than cluttering up tables and working areas.

You will need a large flat-backed basket, some blocks of dried flower foam, some reindeer moss, dried hydrangea heads, glycerined eucalyptus and beech leaves, blue and green agastache (hyssop), poppy seed heads, some seed heads of either *Nigella orientalis* or *N. damascena* (love-in-the-mist), dried blue delphiniums, pale pink helichrysum (straw flower) heads, some gold ribbon and a hot glue gun.

Once again, a little advance preparation is useful. Firstly, you will need some bread rolls, which must be dried in the same way as for the decorated bread board (see page 94) and some small home-made hessian sacks filled with sheets of lasagne, pasta shells and cinnamon sticks, all of which are held in place with strategic dabs of glue from a hot glue gun. You could use other ingredients from your store cupboard (pantry), but the cinnamon gives a delicious smell to the arrangement if you break up the sticks before inserting them in the sacks. This scent can always be increased by bruising the sticks in the sack later on or by adding a few drops of cinnamon essential oil. Finally, prepare some tiny baskets by pushing a small piece of dowelling through the base of each one so it can be stuck into the dried flower foam, then fill each basket with some of the reindeer moss.

Fill the basket with blocks of dried flower foam, then cover the foam with the hydrangea heads. Next, you must insert the glycerined eucalyptus and beech leaves to give the shape of your design. Eucalyptus can easily be air dried, but it comes out a much paler

The Flat-backed Bread Basket continues the theme of using kitchen ingredients for kitchen decorations, including sheets of dried lasagne and dried bread rolls.

blue colour, whereas it becomes a good strong green when left to dry for several days in equal quantities of water and glycerine. When treated in the same way, the beech leaves turn a lovely greeny-bronze and become very glossy.

When this foliage is in place, push the baskets into position, using the little pieces of dowelling to hold them firm, and glue in the hessian sacks of ingredients. Now you can add the bread rolls – either glue them into position or drill a small hole in each dried roll and glue in a small piece of dowelling to act as a stem. The flowers come next – add some of the blue and green agastache, which has a wonderful aniseedy-minty smell, is a very useful shape for flower arranging and has the added bonus of being easy to grow in the garden. Insert some poppy seed heads and the nigella seed heads. Finally, to fill in the small spaces that are inevitably left, use tiny amounts of the delphiniums and helichrysum heads. As I am such a ribbon addict I added some old gold taffeta ribbon wired into loops, but it is not obligatory if you don't share my obsession.

The Dining Room

♣

If you have a separate dining room you might like to make some herbal or spicy arrangements and decorations specially for it, and can really go to town on them. After all, most people only use their dining rooms in the evening (apart from Sunday lunch-times), so you can make something for the dining room that you would tire of, or feel swamped by, in other rooms that you use more often.

EXOTIC TABLE CENTREPIECE

If you are thinking of making a table centrepiece, it should be fairly small or it will get in the way of more important things such as food, glasses and cutlery (silverware)! Always remember to make table centrepieces fairly low otherwise they will block a guest's view of the person sitting opposite them – peering round an immense collection of gladioli can

The Exotic Table Centrepiece and the Spiced Pot Pourri
behind it are both ideal for the dining room as they smell
aromatic without being overpowering.

———— · ————

reduce the entire party to giggles and does not promote sensible and stimulating conversation.

This table centrepiece would also be a good talking point, as some of the guests may not recognize all the ingredients and the soft smells of the beeswax mingling with the coffee, vanilla, ginger and cinnamon will add a lovely perfume to the room without being an overpowering scent that puts everyone off their food. To make it, you will need an oval dark cork mat for the base, three green frogs (plastic fixtures with prongs that are used to hold flower foam in place), one large and two small beeswax candles, five small home-made hessian sacks, whichever spicy ingredients you fancy – I used unshelled walnuts, vanilla pods (beans), cinnamon sticks, coffee beans and fresh root ginger – pine cones and bay leaves, plus your hot glue gun which should have become an old friend by now.

Glue the plastic frogs on to the middle of the cork mat, leave to dry and then push the candles on to them. Beeswax is very soft so you will be able to do this easily, but if you use ordinary candles you'll have to use special candleholders. Make the small hessian sacks and fill them with the spicy ingredients, glueing them into place wherever necessary – you will certainly have to glue the root ginger, coffee beans and walnuts in place to stop them spilling all over the table at the wrong moment. Very firmly glue the sacks into position on the cork base and wait for them to dry, then test them to ensure they are strongly secured. If necessary, add some more glue and test again. As a finishing touch, glue in some pine cones and bay leaves to fill the gaps between the sacks.

SPICED POT POURRI

Another way of adding some subtle perfume to the dining room is to make an interesting pot pourri with a suitably culinary fragrance so it can blend into the general agreeable aroma, rather than having a very strong perfume that hits you as soon as you walk into the dining room and refuses to go away. Again, I used a mixture of spices and spice oils to achieve the desired effect.

1 handful dried *Nigella damascena* seed heads
1 handful dried creamy white xeranthemum daisies
1 handful dried pale yellow helichrysum (straw flower) heads
1 handful broken cinnamon sticks
1 handful whole and broken star anise
1 handful root ginger, chopped
1 handful whole nutmegs
1 handful small pine cones
5 ml (1 tsp) powdered orris root
10 ml (2 tsp) mixed spicy oils

Place the nigella seed heads, xeranthemum daisies, helichrysum (straw flower) heads and orris root in a very large ceramic or glass mixing bowl and stir thoroughly until well combined. Add the mixed spicy oils (I used cinnamon and allspice) and stir together really thoroughly, using a metal spoon. Now add the cinnamon sticks, star anise, root ginger, whole nutmegs and small pine cones and stir again, then tip the whole pot pourri into a large plastic bag (ensure it doesn't have any holes in it) and shake well. Tie the top tightly together and leave in a warm dark place for a week or two, shaking it whenever the thought occurs to you. Then pour the pot pourri into a suitable container to display it. I have used a wooden bowl which not only suits the style of the pot pourri but also lengthens its life because it soaks up some of the oils. However, it does mean you will never again be able to use it for food, so be warned before you get out your favourite salad bowl!

INDIVIDUAL POSIES

When you are entertaining, it is often the small touches that your guests remember rather than the complicated nature of your recipes or the excellence of the wine. For example, a tiny posy set beside each plate will make the table look extra pretty and ensure each guest has something to remind them of the occasion. These little posies are quick to make and very effective. Spice posies like this originate from Austria and Switzerland and can be as simple or as complicated as you like. The frills can be made by gathering a ruffle of material into a circle or by using

*Marking each place setting with an individual posy is an
ideal way of decorating a dining table when you are very
short of space and a central arrangement would be too big.*

a small paper doiley. Alternatively you can buy ready-made frills such as the one shown in the photograph.

There are several methods of making these little posies but one of the easiest is to work from a base of *Limonium dumosa* (statice or sea lavender). To make each posy, wire together a small bunch with fairly long stems and pass it through the hole in the centre of the frill (or make a hole in the centre of your paper doiley). Then push the frill up the bunch until it is tightly wedged in position – if using a doiley you will have to wrap some wire round it to hold it in

place. Cover the stalks (stems) with some gutta percha, which is a sticky florists' tape, or bind them tightly with a length of toning ribbon to make them look more attractive. Now, using a hot glue gun, add various ingredients to the top of the posy – I chose baby rosebuds, some miniature poppy seed heads, star anise and some pearl beads. When the posy looks full, tie some bows with long trailing streamers around the base of the posy. I chose a light and dark pink taffeta ribbon but you can use any colour you wish to match the rest of your table.

PEONY-FILLED BOX

If your dining room is large enough to house a side table or sideboard, not only does it provide useful storage space but also the ideal surface for displaying flowers and other decorative objects. This dried peony arrangement is simple but very effective and has been much admired over the years. I have moved it from room to room in our house, added new flowers and changed the ribbons, but I shall always be very fond of it, partly because I collect antique boxes but also for its wonderful simplicity of design.

You will need some blocks of dried flower foam, sprigs of air-dried bay leaves, peony flowers, aster flowers, ribbon and lace, as well as the box. First fill the box with dried flower foam – if it is an antique box then, whatever you do, don't glue a plastic frog in the bottom or use some sticky modelling clay to hold the foam in place but, instead, just wedge it into the box so it cannot move. There is no need to cover the foam with hydrangea heads or statice as you will be filling the box full of peonies. First arrange some of the bay stems in the flower foam to make the basic shape of the design. Carefully ease the peony flowers as open as possible without dislodging any petals or damaging the flowers and arrange them in the foam, in a shape that complements the box. Now place some stems of dried asters between the bay and the peonies – this adds a lovely delicate touch to the collection. Finally add some loops of ribbon or lace, depending on the style of the room which will contain the box – I added some burgundy and ivory ribbon this time but in the past have used antique ivory lace and broad moiré ribbons.

TERRACOTTA BASKET

Another suggestion for a side table or sideboard is this lovely basket with its terracotta colour scheme, including dried pomegranates and large cassia sticks. Cassia is a cheaper form of cinnamon and produces large, coarse sticks which are not very good for cookery but are stunning in flower arrangements. If you are going to place this arrangement on a side table in a corner, only the front will be visible so you can make the arrangement flat at the back.

*My Peony-filled Box still looks spectacular, even though
I have had it for several years. If you decorate an antique
box, take care not to damage it in the process.*

*The colours of this Terracotta Basket seem particularly
suitable for a dining room, and it is filled with ingredients
that will add a gentle fragrance to the room.*

To make the basket, you will need the basket, some dried flower foam, burgundy coloured hydrangea heads, bunches of *Achillea filipendula* (fernleaf yellow yarrow), millet, glycerined beech leaves, green agastache (hyssop), some natural poppy seed heads, dried pomegranates mounted on sticks (just push the pointed end of the stick into the pomegranate), some rusty red broom bloom, long cassia sticks and a suitable ribbon.

Fill the basket with the flower foam, then cover its surface with the hydrangea heads. Now begin to add the flowers, millet, beech leaves and poppy seed heads, and fill in any gaps with the dried pomegranates. To lighten the feel of the basket, push in some sprays of the rusty red bloom broom and some long sticks of cassia. Alternatively, you can wire up bundles of cinnamon sticks, leaving a long leg with which to push them into the arrangement. For the finishing touch I added a rusty-terracotta hessian bow, wired into loops at each side of the handle.

THE LIVING ROOM

♣

Whether your living room is a family room full of clutter and chatter, or a peaceful room used only by adults for reading and other well-behaved activities, it is a very important room in the house and so needs some special arrangements and decorative features. There are bound to be some ideal spots for flower arrangements and other herb and spice creations which will help to give the room a deliciously soft and subtle fragrance.

OLD-FASHIONED CLOVE POMANDERS

If you are lucky enough to have a fireplace in your living room it is the ideal place for a scented arrangement as the warmth from the fire will bring out its fragrance – pine cones are especially suitable. Having said that, please take care not to place anything combustible like dried flowers too near a blazing fire because they could easily become part of it!

I love clove pomanders and really enjoy making them and, as I like to have them in the house all year round and not just at Christmas, I decided that decorating a basket with them would be an unusual way of using them.

I make my pomanders from apples, although you can use oranges, lemons, limes and other citrus fruits, but the important thing is to ensure that each fruit is fresh and in perfect condition – don't be tempted into thinking this is a good way of using up the contents of a neglected or forgotten fruit bowl because badly bruised or wizened apples will still look awful when they are pomanders. Before you begin, be warned that this is a rather messy project and is best done with a towel across your lap and a wet cloth to wipe your hands on every now and then. Don't do it near anything that could be ruined by flying fruit juice!

Cover each apple with cloves, placing them as close together as possible. If you are using citrus fruits, their skin is much thicker than it is on apples so you will have to pierce each hole with a tapestry (needlepoint) or knitting needle before you insert the clove, making it a much longer job. If you don't do this, the cloves will break in half and be wasted.

Continue to stud each fruit with cloves until you have made as many pomanders as you wish, then leave them on a warm surface to dry for about two weeks. I usually place my pomanders on a suitable radiator, but you could also use a boiler cupboard or similarly warm spot. Check the fruit regularly and turn it if necessary to help the drying process. The smell of these pomanders will not be as strong as when they are rolled in orris root powder and left to dry but I find this method works every time and you can add drops of your chosen fragrance, such as allspice oil, when the fruit has dried out.

The basket was decorated by wiring up some loops of a green shot taffeta ribbon and then glueing them to the basket. When the glue was dry, I carefully added the pomanders, using plenty of glue and holding them in position until they had set in place. I also added some loops of lace, pieces of dried hydrangea and a little broom bloom in its natural colour. To fill the basket, I used a mixture of pine cones which I scented with various spicy fragrances, such as nutmeg, cinnamon, coriander and aniseed essential oils. I usually scent cones individually rather than all together in a plastic bag because the cones are so porous that the top ones soak up all the oil and the bottom ones remain unscented. Whenever the pine cones start to lose their scent you can revive them by adding more drops of the appropriate essential oil.

PRESSED HERB PICTURE

A very traditional way to display herbs is to press them and then make a pressed herb picture from them. The joy of making pictures like this is that they can be as big or as small as you wish, according to the plant material you have and the place where they will eventually be displayed. Such pictures look particularly good in living rooms but do try to hang them in a shadowy position as strong sunlight will

———————— · ————————

You can make clove pomanders from a variety of fruits, but I chose apples to decorate this basket, which I filled with pine cones scented with essential oils.

soon make your carefully pressed herbs and flowers fade to a shadow of their former selves. Our home is so old that that windows are very small, so my pressed flower pictures last for ten years or more with no problems of fading. My sister's house, on the other hand, is very modern with large south-facing windows so many of her rooms are most unsuitable for pressed herb or flower pictures and dried arrangements as they fade quite quickly.

This pressed herb picture has been made on a silk background and it does require plenty of patience to piece it all together, but a simpler version could be just as attractive, perhaps arranged on cream card and in a smaller size. There are many ways of displaying pressed herbs – you could take a botanical approach, for instance, and show all the sections of the plant, or you could arrange rows of herbs like cigarette cards within the picture and label each one.

Obviously you will need to prepare the ingredients for this picture long before you make it, because you must first press the herbs. If you wish, you can include certain flowers, such as pansies, nasturtiums and violas, under the heading of 'herbs', which will add extra colour to your picture. Pick perfect examples of the herbs and flowers and transfer them to the press as soon as possible. You can buy a suitable flower press from a craft shop or children's shop, but it will probably contain some pieces of corrugated cardboard which you must throw away as otherwise you will end up with corrugated pressed flowers and herbs! Instead, fill it with 20 pieces of good-quality blotting paper interspersed with thick pads of newspaper. Place a sheet of newspaper in the bottom of the press, then put a sheet of blotting paper on top. It is now ready to receive the flowers. Trim off any stalks (stems) or pieces that stick out, then place a few of the herbs on the blotting paper with space between each flower or leaf. Cover this layer with another sheet of blotting paper, followed by more newspaper, then another sheet of blotting

———————————— . ————————————

If you are going to make a Pressed Herb Picture, make sure you hang it away from strong sunlight, otherwise it will fade. The Sentimental Lavender Basket is sitting below it.

paper and some more herbs. Continue to fill the press in this way until you have used up all the blotting paper and newspaper, then screw down the press and stick on a label stating the date and contents. Leave the press in a warm dry place for about six weeks, then unscrew it and carefully remove the herbs. You have to be patient with this process, because if you remove the herbs before they are ready they will just turn mouldy.

To make this picture you will need a square frame, some glass and a hardboard back to fit it, a mount, piece of silk, piece of rubber foam, the pressed herbs and flowers, some latex adhesive and a fine needle. Tape the piece of silk, having trimmed it so it is slightly smaller than the mount, to the back of the mount, making it as taut as possible and with the right side visible through the mount. Trim the piece of foam to the same size as the hardboard backing. Place the backing on a flat surface, put the piece of foam on top and cover it with the mount, with the wrong side down. You can then arrange the herbs and flowers as you wish in the silk revealed by the mount. In the photograph the pressed herb picture is in the shape of a wreath or ring, but you could easily arrange the pressed herbs in a semi-circle or spray. I find it best to position the leaves first to form the basic shape, then to add the daintier pieces of herb and finally to arrange the flowers on top, but without sticking any of them in position – that comes later. The herbs for this picture include silverweed leaves (used wrong side up to show their silvery undersides), alchemilla (lady's mantle), fennel, borage, 'Canary Bird' roses, violas, astrantia (masterwort) flowers, marjoram and lavender.

When you are happy with the arrangement, cover it with its sheet of glass to protect it from curious fingers or sudden draughts (drafts), and go off and do something else for a couple of hours. When you return to the picture later it will be with a fresh eye, so you can instantly see if there are any changes you wish to make. Having checked the picture, you can now stick down the ingredients. They will be held quite firmly in place by the frame, so there's no need to ruin the picture by smothering everything in glue.

Instead, using the tip of the needle to produce tiny dabs of the latex adhesive, just anchor everything in place and leave it to dry. Replace the glass on top of the picture, fit the frame on top and turn everything upside down. Fix the hardboard backing on to the frame with a professional framer's staple gun or by inserting small panel pins (brads) at 4-cm (1½-in) intervals. Tape all around the inside of the frame at the place where the frame meets the hardboard to protect the picture from damp or mould. If this all sounds too complicated, you can take your finished picture, well glued down and protected by its sheet of glass, to a professional picture framer and ask him or her to finish it off for you. Incidentally, if you make the design on cream card the whole arrangement will be much easier to frame as it won't need the foam backing and you can use a straightforward photograph frame instead of a picture frame.

SENTIMENTAL LAVENDER POT POURRI

I have always been keen on lavender as a plant and as a fragrance, but since writing a small book on the subject I've become a complete addict. The oil of lavender is a wonderful product that is invaluable in the home. Its medicinal properties are numerous and, as far as I'm concerned, one of its very best uses is that it helps to promote calm and peaceful sleep. Even during the day, if I'm feeling overwrought for some reason, I find a spray of cologne made from real lavender oil is very soothing – I wouldn't be without it! There are many sources of lavender oil and other lavender-related products, but do take care to choose a reputable one as the quality can vary considerably from one firm to another.

Since lavender has such a calming effect I thought it might be a good choice for a living room pot pourri because it would help to induce an air of serenity, as well as a lovely scent. You can alter the quantities of the pot pourri according to the size of the container you wish to fill, and also how much or how little of the ingredients you have, but if you double up the ingredients in this recipe don't forget to do the same with the orris root and essential oil.

1 handful dried lavender flowers

1 handful dried tiny rosebuds

1 handful dried green hydrangea florets

5 ml (1 tsp) powdered orris root

5 ml (1 tsp) lavender essential oil

Place all the ingredients in a large ceramic or glass mixing bowl and mix well together using a metal spoon. When all the ingredients have been thoroughly incorporated, turn the mixture into a large plastic bag without any holes, give it a good shake and tie the top tightly. Leave in a warm dark place for a week or two, shaking the bag whenever you remember to do so, then tip the pot pourri into your chosen container. When the smell starts to fade you can easily revive it by placing all the ingredients in the mixing bowl, adding more lavender essential oil and storing it in a plastic bag for a couple of weeks in the same way as before.

SENTIMENTAL LAVENDER BASKET

I also decorated the basket that would hold the pot pourri, partly because I wanted to carry the theme of lavender through to the container and partly because I like all the objects in my living room, whether they are pictures or ornaments, to have a sentimental association. In this case, the bunches of lavender wired around the outside of the basket were given to me by a delightful Japanese lady who did the translation for the Japanese edition of my lavender book. When I was in Japan recently she contacted me and presented me with a lovely box wrapped in the beautiful way all Japanese gifts are – it contained some strikingly dark blue lavender and some lovely lavender dolls and fans. Thoughtfulness like that stays in the memory, so I decided to incorporate her gift into the basket so it could sit on our piano and remind me of Jersey (where my sister lives and the lavender came from) and Japan at the same time!

Once you begin to make your own pot pourris you will probably become fascinated by the process and want to keep experimenting with new mixtures and fragrances.

———————— • ————————

It is very easy to make – all you need is a suitable basket, some bunches of dried lavender which you have first wired to hold them together and then tied with some attractive ribbon and some dried pale pink roses wired into a spray and then tied with more ribbon. Glue the bunches of lavender around the rim of the basket, then glue a spray of the roses around the base of one handle. If you are going to place the basket in front of a wall you need only arrange the roses on the side that will face the room. Incidentally, if you find there isn't enough pot pourri to fill your basket you can cheat by filling most of it with crumpled tissue paper or newspaper and then covering it with the pot pourri.

HELICHRYSUM (STRAW FLOWER) AND BAY TOPIARY TREE

A topiary tree is an ideal way of displaying a free-standing flower arrangement as it has its own base and doesn't need to take up valuable space on a table. Instead, it looks marvellous in a hall, living room or even on a wide bend on the stairs, and will always attract appreciative comments.

I used bay leaves as the base foliage for this tree, because it is a quick way to fill up the tree and looks marvellous. The best way to use bay is to cut small branches from the tree and air dry them, then you can either use them as they are or cut off individual leaves. As well as the foliage, you will also need a terracotta flowerpot or other container for the base, some quick-drying cement, a 46-cm (18-in) long stick (a cut-down broom handle is ideal), a dried flower foam ball 20 cm (8 in) in diameter, blocks of the dried flower foam, dried carthamus (safflower) heads, some creamy *Limonium dumosa* or sea lavender, dozens of good-quality multi-coloured helichrysum (straw flower) heads wired on to 10-cm (4-in) medium-gauge wires and plenty of cinnamon or cassia sticks. It takes a lot of material to fill a topiary tree so don't underestimate how much you will need.

Fill the flowerpot or container three-quarters full of the cement and push the stick firmly into the middle, then leave it to dry slowly for at least a

Before you begin work on the Helichrysum (straw flower) and Bay Topiary Tree, it is a good idea to consider the colour scheme of the intended room and plan accordingly.

couple of days. When the cement is thoroughly dry, push the flower foam ball on to the top of the stick (you may find it easier to make a starter hole in the foam before you do this) so it is held firmly in place and is about halfway through the centre of the foam ball. Fill the top of the container with the flower foam until it is level with the rim, then arrange the bay leaves all over the flower foam in the base of the container and all over the foam ball at the top.

Carthamus is a sort of thistle and is very useful as a filler in larger arrangements because of its size and the interesting shape of the flower heads. Push the carthamus heads all over the ball, followed by the statice, then add the helichrysums to both the ball and the base. Finally, push the cassia or cinnamon sticks into the base of the pot to give some scent.

POMANDER AND PEONY BOX

A final idea for the living room is a pretty box with a decoration on the lid. You could use an antique wooden box for this, but it does seem a shame to glue things on to something that is valuable, so try to find a box that is attractive but not worth any money. I used a papier mâché box but you could use a box sold for packaging a gift.

The centrepiece of the design is another clove pomander, but this time one made from an orange and therefore fairly large. Make the pomander in the same way as for the apple one (see page 104), but puncture the holes in the skin with something sharp before inserting the cloves or they will break. You will also need some peach and lace ribbon, a wide strip of lace, dried peonies, peachy-pink roses, apricot

Limonium sinuatum, some pinky broom bloom, some wired bunches of thyme, light-gauge florist's wire and a hot glue gun. Wrap the wide strip of lace around the outside of the box and glue the two pieces together at the back of the box. Wire the peach and lace ribbon into long loops and glue them on to the lid of the box. Now glue the pomander on top of the lid, using plenty of glue and holding it in place until the glue sets. Add the peonies next, followed by the peachy-pink roses. Fill any gaps with the statice and broom bloom.

This kind of arrangement inevitably gets dusty after a while, but wielding a duster on it will cause irreparable damage. Instead, I find that a hair-drier set on cool and at its slowest speed blows the dust away very efficiently.

The Pomander and Peony Box would be a lovely addition to any room but is especially attractive in a living room. Try not to damage the box if it is an antique.

———————— • ————————

THE BEDROOMS

♣

If you are lucky, your bedroom is a haven of peace that you can escape to at the end of each day. In most bedrooms there is limited space for large arrangements but small baskets and other containers can sit on dressing tables or window sills and add a touch of the country, no matter where you live.

CUP OF ROSES

If space is at a premium in a bedroom then a small dainty arrangement is ideal. This Limoges cup and saucer makes a very pretty container. You will need some dried flower foam, a green plastic frog if you wish to glue it to the bottom of the cup, dried hydrangea florets or statice, dried or glycerined gypsophila (baby's breath), dried asters wired into small bunches and some dried roses.

First, you must fix the dried flower foam into the cup – glue a green plastic frog to the bottom of the cup to hold the foam in place, tape the foam to the cup with some florist's tape or simply wedge in enough foam so it stays put. Now hide the top of the foam by covering it with pieces of dried hydrangea or some statice. If you use enough roses you need not cover the foam at all because the roses themselves will hide it.

Now arrange the roses in the cup – choose fairly small flowers as larger ones may be too big for the scale of the cup and saucer. Keep the shape of the arrangement tidy, then add small bunches of dried asters, which look very fresh and charming. You could also use some dried or glycerined gypsophila depending on the colour scheme of the arrangement. If you wish you can also add some pearl or ribbon loops but for once I chose not to!

LARKSPUR, HONEYSUCKLE AND STAR ANISE
POT POURRI

A pot pourri mix is another excellent addition to the bedroom as it is wonderful to be greeted by wafts of a beautiful scent whenever you open the bedroom door. This might be a room where you would prefer to use a ready-mixed perfume oil in your pot pourri rather than a blend of different essential oils.

1 handful dried pink larkspur flowers
1 handful dried blue larkspur flowers
1 handful dried white larkspur flowers
2 handfuls dried pink rosebuds
1 handful dried cream statice (see lavender) flowers
1 handful broken star anise
30 ml (2 tbsp) powdered orris root
15 ml (3 tsp) honeysuckle oil
sprays of dried pink larkspur and some whole
star anise to decorate the basket

Mix all the ingredients together in a large ceramic or glass bowl and stir well with a metal spoon. Tip the mixture into a large plastic bag without holes, shake well, secure the top tightly and leave in a warm airy place for a week or two, shaking it whenever you remember to do so. Tip the pot pourri out into a basket or any other container that you have chosen.

For this arrangement, I glued dried pink larkspur and whole star anise to the base of the handles of the basket, then filled the bottom of the basket with crumpled tissue paper, covered it with a pretty lace handkerchief and poured on the pot pourri.

Insomnia is not something that our family has ever suffered from for more than a night or two at a time, but whenever it has occurred it has been very frustrating and I do sympathise with anyone who suffers from it constantly. There are various herbal mixtures that can help to induce sleep but their effectiveness or otherwise is very much a matter of personal experience. Even so, sometimes a so-called old wives' remedy can be better than all the medication in the world, so here are some ideas for mixtures that can be packed into small sachets and placed inside cushions or pillows on the bed.

———————— • ————————

Opposite: Here are two decorations that are suitable for a bedroom – the Cup of Roses and a basket, lined with a lace handkerchief, containing the Larkspur Pot Pourri.

*I like to decorate my herbal sachets and anti-moth bags with
small posies of dried flowers and herbs, even if no one is
going to see them except me and the moths.*

HOP MIXTURE FOR SLEEPLESSNESS

This is a very simple recipe for a sleep-inducing mixture. It works well for some people in these proportions, or the hop flowers can be used on their own.

1 handful dried hop flowers
½ handful dried marjoram
½ handful dried catnip flowers

Mix all the ingredients together in a large bowl and use the mixture to stuff a large sachet which you can quickly make from a piece of cotton. Sew the raw edges of the sachet opening together, and place this sachet inside a pillowcase, with the pillow, to prevent the pollen irritating the nasal passages.

HERBS RECOMMENDED FOR SLEEPLESSNESS

My most successful remedy for insomnia, or one of those awful nights when you can't stop your brain churning over problems or anxieties, is to place a few drops of lavender essential oil on a piece of cloth and place it on the pillow near my head. Dropping the oil directly on to the pillow may leave grease marks. You can also fill small sachets with a mixture of dried lavender flowers, lily of the valley flowers and primroses, all of which are recommended for their soothing qualities, and tuck them into your pillow. However, I find the oil on its own works best for me as lavender flowers make me sneeze.

Other herbs which are useful in the treatment of insomnia include basil, camomile and heartsease. However, these are really only suitable for the occasional sleepless night, and any serious problems should always be treated by a qualified doctor.

HERBAL SACHETS

Another use for sachets in the bedroom is to scent bed linen and towels, clothes that are airing and those in drawers and cupboards (closets). I would choose lavender sachets for this purpose, but there are many other wonderfully scented herbs and spices to choose from as well. Make some small sachets from a plain or printed fabric and fill them with a dried herbal mixture of your choice, secure the top of each sachet with an elastic band and trim with ribbons or sprays of dried flowers. Even if they aren't going to be seen because they'll be sitting in a drawer, I enjoy making these sachets look as pretty as possible and they are marvellously useful gifts.

MOTH DETERRENTS

For years now I have been waging my own personal war against moths – they spoilt many much-loved woollen clothes before I started to get my own back by placing a special anti-moth sachet in every suitable drawer and cupboard in the house. No one seems to use moth balls any more, which is probably just as well because they have such a pungent and characteristic smell, but there are much sweeter-smelling ways of combating these flying foes. If you make up this mixture you can again fill little sachets or sacks with it and hang them up in wardrobes (closets) or leave in drawers. Don't be so keen to start your vendetta against moths that you fill the sachets before the mixture is ready, otherwise the essential oil could stain the sachets.

1 handful dried lavender flowers
1 handful dried thyme
1 handful dried marjoram
1 handful dried basil
20 ml (4 tsp) powdered orris root
5 ml (1 tsp) lavender essential oil

Mix together all the ingredients in a large ceramic or glass mixing bowl with a metal spoon. Tip into a large plastic bag without holes, shake well and secure the top tightly and leave in a warm airy place for at least a week, shaking it whenever you remember to do so, until all the oil has been absorbed.

You can easily substitute one herb for another in this recipe, although the lavender is a must because moths can't stand the smell of it. Apparently moths have very delicate noses and steer clear of anything with a strong fragrance, so choose any herbs that smell good to you but nasty to moths!

TEDDY PICTURE

Dried flowers are not usually put in children's bedrooms for obvious reasons of potential demolition, and also because some of the ingredients could be poisonous if the child decides to eat them. Another reason is that some dried flowers can be quite sharp or contain sharp items, such as rose thorns. So you should keep dried arrangements out of harm's way in the adults' bedrooms, but there's no reason why you couldn't display a dried herb picture in a nursery. In this arrangement, a teddy bear is sitting in the middle of a border of herbs, to make a sweet picture for a young child's room.

The teddy was already printed on the card, so I just glued the herbs all round it using a latex adhesive (see pages 104-8). The flowers and foliage included silverweed leaves, fennel foliage, alchemilla (lady's mantle) flowers, rue leaves (the 'Jackman's Blue' variety), miniature rosebuds, daisies and borage flowers. Once the flowers are glued in place you can either frame the picture yourself or take it to a professional framer.

This Teddy Picture, made from pressed herbs, is a charming decoration for a child's bedroom and would be suitable for a small boy or girl. It is also a good gift for a child.

———————— • ————————

DRIED POSY

If you want to stick to the idea of roses but fancy a less formal arrangement, you can tie ribbon round a hand-held bunch of roses and add some alchemilla (lady's mantle). I have to own up and admit that I tied about three-quarters of these roses into a bunch, with some alchemilla, then wound some wire round the stems followed by a ribbon. Then, to give the bunch a better shape, I used a hot glue gun to add some bay leaves, more roses and more tiny pieces of alchemilla (lady's mantle). I then decided that the stems looked rather sparse and glued more into the bunch – I'm all in favour of taking the easy way out provided the end result looks as good as possible!

Like the other dried arrangements in this book, this Dried Posy of roses and alchemilla (lady's mantle) can be gently dusted with a hair-drier on the lowest setting.

———— · ————

THE CONSERVATORY

♣

Not all of us are fortunate enough to have a conservatory but the ideas in this section can be used for any room in the house, provided it is not damp and unheated (dried flowers and herbs like to be cosseted and kept warm and dry). I'd love a conservatory to take some of the plants bursting out of the greenhouse and also give us somewhere to sit when it's too windy in the garden.

LAVENDER AND HERB TREE

As well as all the exotic plants that usually live in a conservatory, an elaborate topiary tree can look very effective. This tall version takes a lot of plant material but looks stunning when it is finished, so is worth the time and energy involved. The base is a flower-pot and, as with all the other topiary trees in this book (see pages 110 and 136–8), has been three-quarters filled with cement, with a full-length broom handle embedded in the cement and left to dry. Impale a dry flower foam ball, 20 cm (8 in) in diameter, on the top of the handle and fill up the gap between the cement and the rim of the flowerpot with blocks of dried flower foam. For the plant material, you will need green *Limonium dumosa* (statice or sea lavender) which has been sprayed a mossy green using floral spray colour, some green honesty seed heads, and small bundles of marjoram, agastache (hyssop) and lavender. You will also need some small balls of lavender, which I made by wrapping pieces of wide wired ribbon around handfuls of lavender flowers. Alternatively, you could make these lavender balls by cutting out small circles of material in a suitable colour and placing a clump of lavender flowers in the middle of them. Gather up the edges of each one and hold them together with an elastic band, then wire the top of the bundle tightly, leaving a long leg sticking out with which to impale the bundle on the tree.

Cover the foam ball and the foam in the base with a layer of the statice, then add the other ingredients in the order given above. When you are happy with the result, add the lavender balls.

The Lavender and Herb Tree was designed for a conservatory but would look just as good in a hallway or standing on a bend in the stairs. The lavender gives it a lovely smell.

————— · —————

HAMPER OF HERBS

Casual flower arrangements, such as this hamper of dried herbs, can look very effective when carefully placed in a strategic position around the house. I chose the mixture of herbs for their blend of colour and shape. The *Atriplex hortensis* is a very useful plant which is sometimes known as orache, and its burgundy and green tones blend in with many colour schemes. The attractive seeds make a good contrast in shape to the *Agastache foeniculum* (hyssop) flowers, which are strong and pointed. The ambrosinia (ambrosia) is a delicate green filler which doesn't look strong enough on its own but blends well with other colours and shapes. Finally, the little yellow bobbles of the tansy flowers make a good bright contrast and nestle well into the other foliage. You will also need several blocks of dried flower foam.

To begin the arrangement, wedge the foam into the hamper. In this case, the base of the hamper is curved so I had to cut the foam to fit it. Start to fill the hamper with the dried flowers and herbs, following the order in which I listed them in the previous paragraph. Group each herb or flower in small bunches to give a solid-looking arrangement with clumps of particular colours, rather than a sparse-looking wispy one. You can, of course, replace any of the plants I mention here with whatever you have dried from the garden, but do try to have some variation in colour and shape.

BESOM BROOM

With the same natural theme in mind as I used for the herby hamper, I thought an old-fashioned besom broom would be a suitable decoration for a garden room or conservatory. You can still buy brooms of this sort from some suppliers and, incidentally, they are excellent sweepers as well as being most attractive! I decorated the handle in a simple way to make it an interesting talking point.

As well as the broom, you will need some wide ribbon, plus some bunches of *Atriplex hortensis* (orache) and agastache (hyssop) and a hot glue gun. I made a large bow from some cotton tartan ribbon that came from America, but any casual style of ribbon would do, such as gingham. Having made the bow, glue it on to the handle, then glue on the bunches of dried flowers and herbs. I liked the casual simplicity of this design, but you could add more plant material for a more formal effect if you wished.

INSECT REPELLENTS

It's lovely eating *al fresco*, whether it is in a conservatory with all the windows wide open or out on a patio or veranda, but as far as I'm concerned the big drawback is the insects that seem determined to join in. If moths aren't dive-bombing the candles then mosquitoes are making a meal of your arms or wasps are trying to eat the dessert. Some people attract insects more than others and I seem to be plagued by mosquitoes in particular, so I'm always

This Hamper of Herbs and Besom Broom have a nice old-fashioned look to them, and I especially like the muted spicy colours of the dried herbs in the hamper.

very interested in any herbal remedies that deter insects and am willing to try anything that promises to annoy them as much as they annoy me.

I am reliably informed that one of the most effective insect repellents is garlic. Many people who live in the Mediterranean wonder why people in other countries suffer so badly from insect bites while they remain blissfully unaffected – the answer has to be in the amount of garlic they consume. In 1649 the herbalist Nicholas Culpeper wrote that it was an excellent remedy against mad dogs and other venomous creatures, and it seems they don't like the smell of onions either. So, if you want to repel insects, rub any uncovered parts of your body with a cut onion or crushed garlic and you will be assured of a trouble-free evening. It will be a lonely one too, as no one will sit anywhere near you!

Other less dramatic (and more sociable) remedies include rubbing lemon juice on your arms and legs (or any other uncovered bits), rubbing lavender essential oil on your skin (blend it first with a little sweet almond oil) or burning lavender- or lemon-scented candles. Alternatively, you could make sachets of this insect repellent and hang them over the arms of your garden chairs, or put them in cushions.

2 large handfuls dried tansy leaves
2 handfuls dried southernwood leaves and flowers
1 handful dried chopped orange peel
5 cinnamon sticks, broken into small pieces
1 handful cloves
4 or 5 drops lavender essential oil

Place all the dry ingredients in a large ceramic or glass mixing bowl and stir thoroughly with a metal spoon. Add the drops of lavender essential oil and stir again, then use the mixture to fill some calico or hessian sachets.

Combat those small flying foes, such as mosquitoes and other inquisitive insects, with bags filled with insect repellents. They smell much nicer than aerosol killers!

This birdcage has been sawn in half so it can be hung flat
on a wall, but you could easily use a real, but decorative,
wooden or bamboo birdcage instead.

DECORATED BIRDCAGE

Although I don't like the idea of having birds indoors, I do love elaborate old birdcages, so when I saw this ornament I just had to have it. It is like a circular birdcage sawn in half, so it can be hung on a wall, and I thought it would look lovely with roses in it. You could also make flower arrangements in real birdcages – a much kinder use for them, I think, than filling them with live birds.

To make the arrangement, you will need the birdcage, a piece of dried flower foam, dried hydrangea florets, dried peach roses, stems of lavender and pieces of ribbon wired into small loops with legs so they can be pushed into the flower foam. Glue a piece of foam to the base of the cage, but don't make it too large or it will be difficult to cover. Some of the flowers are arranged from behind while others will have to be pushed through the front bars. Cover the foam with the hydrangea florets, then arrange the peach roses working from both the back and front of the cage. To add a lighter touch, insert a few stems of lavender – if you have real difficulty in placing a stem a pair of tweezers can help. As a finishing touch, add a few loops of ribbon.

THE BATHROOM

♣

In this section you will find several recipes for exotic bath preparations as well as some decorative ideas for your bathroom. Perhaps you should make the decorations and then spend lots of time enjoying them from the warm depths of your specially scented bath?

At the end of a long tiring day there is nothing more soothing than a relaxing bath using herbal bath oils, but there is no need to buy expensive perfumed bath oil because these home-made preparations can be just as good if not better. To make them, you will need a variety of essential oils which can be bought in some large chemists or by mail order from a variety of suppliers. Should your enthusiasm for these oils extend beyond the bath treatments and ideas given in this section then it is important to buy a good, authoratitave book on the subject written by an expert, as it is easy to misuse oils and cause problems. Used correctly, however, these natural oils can be of immense help in treating many problems and health ailments.

If you are anything like me, you might make these bath oils full of good intentions about giving them as gifts, and then decide to keep the lot for yourself!

———————— · ————————

Here are some suggestions for herbal bath oils that can help to relax you and will relieve depression and mental fatigue. Some of these bath preparations are not suitable for use by pregnant women, diabetics and epileptics – see the front of the book for more details.

PEPPERMINT BATH OIL

45 ml (3 tbsp) sweet almond oil

10 drops peppermint essential oil

10 drops rosemary essential oil

10 drops juniper essential oil

Pour the sweet almond oil into a small decorative bottle with a screw-top lid or properly fitting stopper and add the essential oils. Replace the lid and shake well. To use, add approximately 15 ml (1 tbsp) of the oil just before you step in the bath and give it a good swish around. You can add it under the running taps but if the water is very hot the essential oils will evaporate too quickly and you won't get the full benefit from them. This peppermint bath oil will give you an excellent invigorating bath if you are feeling tired, low or need to wake yourself up.

BLACK PEPPERCORN BATH

45 ml (3 tbsp) sweet almond oil

30 drops black pepper essential oil

Pour the sweet almond oil into a small decorative bottle with a screw-top lid or properly fitting stopper and add the black pepper essential oil. Replace the lid and shake well. About 15 ml (1 tbsp) in a drawn bath will help to ease aching limbs and muscles.

CARDAMOM, GRAPEFRUIT AND CLARY SAGE BATH MIX

75 ml (5 tbsp) sweet almond oil

20 drops cardamom essential oil

10 drops clary sage essential oil

5 drops grapefruit essential oil

Pour the sweet almond oil into a small decorative bottle with a screw-top lid or properly fitting stopper and add the essential oils. Replace the lid and shake well. Use about 15 ml (1 tbsp) in a drawn bath to invigorate and uplift – grapefruit essential oil is said to aid positive thinking.

What better way to relax at the end of a long, tiring day than to soak your cares away in a scented bath?

·

Sometimes you may not want to be uplifted but instead are just longing for a peaceful soak in the bath. If so, here are some oriental bath oils to add a heady fragrance to your bathing. Don't have the water too hot or the oils will evaporate too fast.

JASMINE AND JUNIPER OIL

45 ml (3 tbsp) sweet almond oil

20 drops jasmine essential oil

10 drops juniper essential oil

Pour the sweet almond oil into a small decorative bottle with a screw-top lid or properly fitting stopper and add the essential oils. Replace the lid and shake well. Use about 15 ml (1 tbsp) in a drawn bath to promote a feeling of optimism and confidence. The juniper will help to ease anxiety and nervous tension, and the oil smells delicious.

GERANIUM, LAVENDER AND ALLSPICE OIL

105 ml (7 tbsp) sweet almond oil

20 drops geranium essential oil

20 drops lavender essential oil

20 drops bergamot (oswego tea) essential oil

7 drops allspice essential oil

Pour the sweet almond oil into a small decorative bottle with a screw-top lid or properly fitting stopper and add the essential oils. Replace the lid and shake well. Use about 15 ml (1 tbsp) in a drawn bath to make you feel on top of the world.

HOP, GINGER AND CARDAMOM OIL

75 ml (5 tbsp) sweet almond oil

5 drops ginger essential oil

10 drops cardamom essential oil

20 drops hop essential oil

Pour the sweet almond oil into a small decorative bottle with a screw-top lid or properly fitting stopper and add the essential oils. Replace the lid and shake well. Use about 15 ml (1 tbsp) in a drawn bath to help you relax – it is very good in a warm bath before you go to bed.

ALLSPICE WARMING BATH OIL

45 ml (3 tbsp) sweet almond oil

5 drops allspice essential oil

10 drops camomile essential oil

5 drops nutmeg essential oil

Pour the sweet almond oil into a small decorative bottle with a screw-top lid or properly fitting stopper and add the essential oils. Replace the lid and shake well. Use about 15 ml (1 tbsp) in a drawn bath to warm and relax you.

If you prefer to use a bubble bath rather than an oil, there are plenty of herbal ways to add enjoyment and bubbles to your bath. Some ecological washing up (dish-washing) liquids are milder than ordinary ones.

ALPINE BUBBLE BATH

200 ml (6 fl oz/3/4 cup) washing up (dish-washing) liquid

200 ml (6 fl oz/3/4 cup) water

5 ml (1 tsp) marjoram essential oil

5 ml (1 tsp) rosemary essential oil

Pour the washing up (dish-washing) liquid (you may wish to use an ecologically sound one) into a large bottle, then add the water and the essential oils. Replace the lid and shake well. To use, pour about 15 ml (1 tbsp) of the mixture into the bath under the running water.

BASIL, GERANIUM AND BERGAMOT (OSWEGO TEA) BUBBLES

300 ml (10 fl oz/1 1/4 cups) washing up (dish-washing) liquid

300 ml (10 fl oz/1 1/4 cups) water

5 ml (1 tsp) geranium essential oil

5 ml (1 tsp) bergamot (oswego tea) essential oil

5 ml (1 tsp) basil essential oil

Pour the washing up (dish-washing) liquid (you may wish to use an ecologically sound one) into a large bottle, then add the water and the essential oils. Replace the lid and shake well. To use, pour about 15 ml (1 tbsp) of the mixture into the bath under the running water.

MASSAGE OILS

Aromatherapy and massage is a fascinating subject, but generally speaking one best dealt with by an expert rather than an enthusiastic amateur. However, if you feel that it may be of interest to you there are plenty of books available for further reading. Self-massage is also useful and if you've got a stiff neck, for example, you could rub it with sweet almond oil mixed with marjoram essential oil, or perhaps grapefruit, lavender or rosemary.

It is important to get the proportion between the carrier oil (the oil with which you dilute the essential oils) and the essential oil(s) right – it should be approximately 15 drops of essential oil to 25 ml (5 tsp) of carrier oil (I would recommend sweet almond oil, which is easily available from most chemists).

There are many oils that will help to soothe aches and pains – why not try a lavender, camomile, eucalyptus or black pepper massage? To treat indigestion or flatulence, try a massage with aniseed, caraway or cardamom oil – fennel, peppermint or orange essential oils also work well. A massage of lavender, jasmine or clary sage helps to reduce

If you are prepared to shop around, you can find some lovely soaps, made from natural ingredients, to go with the bathtime preparations you have made yourself.

discomfort during childbirth. Finally, nervous tension and stress can be alleviated by massaging with melissa, bergamot (oswego tea), lavender, marjoram, peppermint or rosemary essential oils.

TUDOR BATH BAGS

Another way of scenting the bath is to immerse a bag of herbal ingredients in the water. These Tudor bath bags are inspired by Nicholas Culpeper who wrote his famous *Herbal* in 1649 – a modern version is available and has some lovely comments in it. I always enjoy reading it for sheer amusement, never mind the useful information it contains!

1 handful dried lavender flowers
5 or 6 pieces root ginger
small handful dried sage leaves

Mix the herbs together in a large ceramic or glass bowl and use to fill a small hessian, muslin (cheesecloth) or calico sack. This is enough to make one bath bag – increase the ingredients according to the number of bags you want to make. Stitch the top of the bath bag together to stop the contents spilling out and sew long ribbons to it so you can suspend it from the bath taps. The running water should flow over the bag and the ribbon must be long enough to allow the bag to sit in the water once the bath has been drawn. Let the bag infuse for a while, then leave it hanging from the tap while you have your bath.

Culpeper suggests this mixture as a remedy for pains in the head and joints, and for lowness of spirits. The only difference between his recipe and mine is that he suggests drinking it while I prefer to have a bath in it!

Another possibility, based on a suggestion by Gerard in his *Herbal* of 1597, is to fill the bags with dried hellebore leaves. I shall give you the quotation but make no comment.

'...hellebore is good for mad and furious men, for melancholy, dull and heavie persons and briefly for all those that are troubled with black choler and molested with melancholy...'

*If you have plenty of space in the bathroom, such as a wide
windowsill, you can make arrangements of cakes of soap,
herbal sachets and bowls of pot pourri.*

———————— • ————————

ROSEMARY FOOTBATH

Tired and aching feet are something most of us suffer
from at some time or another. There are several herbal
bath infusions that are excellent for treating tired feet
and are very simple to concoct. They are good
presents for people who do a lot of standing.

Take 10 or 15 ml (2 or 3 tsp) of fresh rosemary
leaves to every 240 ml (8 fl oz/1 cup) of boiling water
and leave to infuse in a large bowl for at least 24 hours.
Then pour into an attractive bottle, with a sprig of
rosemary. Add about 240 ml (8 fl oz/1 cup) to a bowl
of hot water when you want to soak your aching feet.

Other herbs that are particularly good for
footbaths include peppermint, eucalyptus and thyme,
all of which can be used fresh in the same way as for
the rosemary footbath.

Another use for an infusion of thyme is suggested
by Culpeper and might be as useful today as it
obviously was in the mid 1660s.

*'...thyme...the infusion of the leaves removes
headache...good for headache due to inebriation...it is
a certain remedy for that troublesome complaint, the
nightmare.'*

SHELL WREATH

This decoration needs a fairly large wreath base to take all the shells. I chose fairly small scallop shells as the larger ones would have been too big.

First you must make small wired bunches of all the ingredients you intend to use. Bundle nine pieces of liquorice (licorice) root together and tie them with raffia, make 7.5-10-cm (3-4-in) long bunches of wheat, lavender, marjoram flowers and *Achillea ptarmica* (sneezewort) – this bunch was tinted with a little soft lavender dye. You will also need some bluey-green hydrangea heads, the shells, the wreath base and our old friend, a hot glue gun.

Using the glue gun, start by attaching the wheat and then the shells to the wreath. Place the bundles of liquorice root between the shells so they are well balanced. Then fill the gaps with the small bunches of the other ingredients that you have already

I chose shells for this bathroom wreath for their obvious watery associations, but also because they are so attractive and their shapes can be so varied.

prepared. Make sure that all the wires on these bunches are hidden and that the ends of the stalks (stems) aren't visible. You could also use ribbon if you wanted to, more shells or a raffia bow.

BATHROOM MIRROR

This pine-framed mirror is 30 x 25 cm (12 x 10 in) but you could easily use a much larger one and continue the decoration all the way round, or just decorate the four corners and leave the rest unadorned. I used the same technique for the mirror as for the wreath, making up small bunches of the flowers beforehand and then glueing everything on to the top of the frame.

You will need liquorice (licorice) roots, bundled up in bunches of nine with some raffia, some *Limonium latifolia* (statice) which has been gently dyed with a liquid dye to increase its natural mauve colour, and some *Achillea ptarmica* (sneezewort) which has been treated in the same way. You will also need some natural poppy seed heads and bunches of dried marjoram and oregano, plus a collection of shells – I used a mixture, including some little starfish. If you don't have a collection of shells that you have picked up on your wanderings along beaches over the years there are many shell shops that sell all manner of interesting bits and pieces.

Start with a ready-framed mirror, but be careful not to get any glue on the main part of the glass as it takes a lot of time to clean off. I began with the statice and just worked my way across the top of the mirror, but the order in which you place the ingredients is not important, just a matter of personal choice. Use plenty of glue but beware those annoying little strands that can drape themselves all over the flowers and shells. They can all be pulled off so it isn't a tragedy if you do get glue on the arrangement, but make sure you remove it all or you'll end up with a very cobwebby effect which may not be what you were after.

——————— • ———————

Opposite: I used a mixture of shells, plus starfish, to decorate the top of the mirror, but you might want to omit the dried herbs if your bathroom gets very steamy.

CELEBRATING

WITH

HERBS AND SPICES

Special occasions deserve special arrangements

and decorations, so here are ideas for

wedding bouquets and posies, a christening

pot pourri and topiary tree, plus topiary

trees, pot pourris and table arrangements

for Christmas.

A HERBAL WEDDING

♣

I find it particularly exciting to use the language of flowers when choosing herbs and flowers for wedding work. The Victorians really raised the language of flowers to an art, but sadly it faded from popularity although more and more florists are now including rosemary (for remembrance) or other herbs in their wedding bouquets again.

Many brides like the idea of keeping their wedding bouquets as mementoes, and they can be preserved by experts either in their original state or taken apart and pressed. However, the main drawback with both methods is that the bouquet has to reach the professional preserver as soon as possible after the wedding otherwise the flowers won't be worth keeping, and usually that sort of detail is likely to be forgotten in the general hubbub and enjoyment of the wedding day. I think the best solution is to choose a bouquet of dried flowers and herbs, which can look just as beautiful as a fresh bouquet and will survive quite happily for a long time without much special treatment (although you should keep it out of strong sunlight and away from damp).

WINTER WEDDING BOUQUET

In some parts of the world, such as Britain, it can be difficult or very expensive to find unusual or brightly coloured fresh flowers in the winter months, so I have designed this dried bouquet to add vivid colour and vibrancy to a winter wedding. The bride and bridesmaids all wore cream dresses, and the bridesmaids had apricot and burgundy sashes.

I made the bouquet the easy way, using a dried flower foam base produced specially for bouquets and shaped like the handle of a skipping rope (there is a ball of flower foam with a plastic handle below it). As a trained florist I am sad to see the gradual decline in the number of wired bouquets, but on the other hand I can appreciate that using these special bases saves a great deal of time (and time is always money). It is also much simpler to teach this method and even a beginner could have a go at a bouquet made in this way. In wired bouquets, on the other hand, each flower has to be individually wired up before the bouquet can be assembled, and all the wire stems are bound together with still more wire before being covered with florist's tape and then ribbon.

To make this bouquet, you will need one of the special dried flower foam bouquet bases which are designed for spray bouquets, some branches of glycerined beech leaves, dried red 'Mercedes' roses and apricot 'Calypso' roses, small bunches of dried oregano and red and apricot satin ribbon to match the colours of the roses. Begin with the beech leaves, cutting them into suitable lengths. Push the longest piece into the base of the foam, then continue to build up the basic shape of the bouquet by placing different sized pieces of the beech all over the foam until you have created an elongated round shape which is the basis of the spray. When you are happy with this shape and all the foam is covered you can move on to the roses. I chose red and apricot roses because the two colours work together very well to give a brilliant, vibrant display. Cut down the rose stems to the desired length and place them throughout the bouquet. Keep the mixture random to avoid straight lines of one colour or the heavy grouping of one colour on one side of the bouquet, which would make it look very unbalanced. As you can see from the photograph, you don't need to use many roses to get the desired effect. To finish off the bouquet, place the small bunches of oregano between the roses and the beech leaves to add a touch of green. Finally, glue some long streamers of apricot and red satin ribbon to the base of the foam.

HERBAL HEAD-DRESS

This head-dress would be suitable either for the bride or a bridesmaid. It is more complicated than the bride's bouquet but it is still simple enough for any nimble-fingered arranger to manage. One of the great bonuses of dried flower wedding work is that you can do it all at your leisure well in advance.

You will need four 30-cm (12-in) heavy-gauge wires, some sticky florist's tape called gutta percha,

You can make this Winter Wedding Bouquet and matching
Herbal Head-dress in advance, and then pack them away
in boxes of tissue paper until they are needed.

reel wire, a hot glue gun, ribbons and the selection of flowers and leaves which, in this case, are the same as I used for the bride's bouquet. Wrap some of the gutta percha round two of the wires to hold them together and do the same with the other pair. Now overlap them in the middle and bind tape along the entire length to produce a wire that is about 50 cm (20 in) long. Measure the head of the bride or bridesmaid, then bend the wire round in a circle. Bend both ends of the wire back on themselves to make loops and interlock them to form a circle. Compare the wire circle with the measurement of the girl's head and adjust it to fit by lengthening or shortening the two wire loops.

Starting just beyond one of the loops, begin to wire on small sprigs of beech leaves and bunches of oregano with the reel wire. Continue all the way round the head-dress until it is full and you have reached the other loop. Cut off the rose stems, leaving only a small amount of stem, then glue each rose individually, with the hot glue gun, into the head-dress. Although, technically speaking, the roses should be wired in as you work along the head-dress, I find that many students accidentally break off the wired-in roses as they work, so this method is much safer.

Finally, cut some long pieces of ribbon, according to the height of the bride or bridesmaid and the length you want the streamers, and tie them in a simple knot across the join where the loops are interlocked. This will ensure the join is covered and remind you of the position of the loops if you need to alter the size of the head-dress on the day itself.

BRIDESMAID'S POSY

I made the bridesmaid's posy in exactly the same way as the bride's bouquet, except that I used a round foam ball and a posy frill around the outside of the flowers. These frills can be bought from florist's wholesalers, craft shops and even some garden centres, and they fit over the foam ball at the point where the ball meets the handle, then are glued into position. Take care to keep the frill visible as you

Here is the Bridesmaid's Posy, made to match the Winter Wedding Bouquet, plus a herbal wedding confetti made from larkspur, rosebuds, lavender and marjoram.

work. If the posy is intended for a very young bridesmaid it is advisable to place a small dab of glue on the end of each stalk before pushing it into the foam as this will help the posy to cope with any rough handling it may get. However, I cannot vouch for this if the bridesmaid decides to bounce her posy against a wall, as a certain young bridesmaid that I know did one day when she was keen to practise her tennis strokes!

WEDDING CONFETTI

Many churches and register offices ban wedding confetti now as it is bad for the environment and causes a lot of extra work when it comes to sweeping it all up. It is far better to throw natural confetti made from rice, rose petals or small flowers. This will do no damage to the surrounding area and looks far prettier than the brightly coloured pieces of paper that are available commercially. Here is my recipe for a herbal wedding mix.

1 measure dried pink larkspur flowers
1 measure dried blue larkspur flowers
1 measure dried white larkspur flowers
1 measure dried pink rose petals or tiny rose buds
1 measure dried lavender flowers
1 measure dried marjoram leaves

Mix all the ingredients in a large ceramic or glass bowl, then store in a sealed bag to keep the damp out. If you want to hand out the confetti to friends and family on the day, it is a lovely idea to pack it into individual bags and decorate them with a bow and some of the dried flowers – for the bag in the photograph I used pink ribbon, sprigs of lavender, pink larkspur and a few small rosebuds.

Not only does this mixture look very pretty, but each of the flowers has a special meaning. In the language of flowers, larkspur means lightness and levity, rosebuds mean pure and lovely, lavender signifies silence (but it smells nice so I included it anyway) and marjoram means health and happiness. So when you use your confetti you will be showering the bride and groom with good wishes in more ways than one!

A Herbal Christening

♣

The theme for this section is a christening, but you could easily adapt the ideas for other celebrations. Herbs and spices can easily play an attractive role in these arrangements and I hope some of these ideas will inspire you to think up other ways of including them in your celebrations.

BEAR TREE

If you are planning a very large family gathering at which you will be serving food you may decide that a buffet is the only way to do it, especially if you don't have a large enough table to fit everyone round. An arrangement in the middle of all the food always looks lovely, and I think this tree with little bears climbing up it complements the theme of the christening and provides an amusing conversation piece.

Fill a small flowerpot base with cement and a fairly short broom handle or interesting branch in the usual way (see page 110). Push a 9-cm (3½-in) diameter dried flower foam ball on the top of the branch or broom handle and fill the space between the cement and the rim of the flowerpot with pieces of dried flower foam. You will also need some reindeer moss, *Limonium dumosa* (statice or sea lavender), several small bears, dried pink and peach roses, sprigs of dried marjoram, small bunches of dried heather, dried bay leaves and a hot glue gun.

Cover the foam in the base with the moss, glueing it in place, then cover the ball on top by pushing in individual sprigs of statice. Now you must glue the bears into position. These bears were jointed, so I could move their heads, arms and legs into any position I wanted. However, if you can only find small bears that are rigid you could make them stand on each others' shoulders instead. Either way, glue them firmly to the trunk and flowerpot so they can't move. Now start covering the ball with the peach and pink roses, marjoram, heather and bay leaves. As well as choosing these ingredients for their appearance, I also considered their meanings according to the language of flowers. Heather symbolizes protection, bay means glory, marjoram means health and

These little bears are busy clambering up the Bear Tree, making it a good decoration for a christening, or any other celebration involving a small child.

———— • ————

happiness and roses are for love – a good christening message for a little baby.

CHRISTENING POSIES

It is a nice idea to give small mementoes to the godparents of your new baby so they will have something that reminds them of his or her christening. A small posy is a good idea for godmothers, using ingredients that match the rest of the christening decorations. For this posy, you will need a posy frill, some dried peach and pink roses, dried heather, dried alchemilla (lady's mantle) flowers, some cloves, florist's tape or gutta percha, some reel wire, a hot glue gun and some ribbons.

*The Christening Posies are lovely mementoes for the baby's
godmothers, and the Christening Pot Pourri will remind
you of the special day for months afterwards.*

———————— · ————————

Take a group of three roses and bind them together
with the wire, fairly high under the flower heads, but
don't cut the wire. Then wrap a circle of heather and
alchemilla flowers around the roses and bind them in
place with the wire. Continue to wrap ingredients
around the flowers already wired together until the
posy is the size and shape you want. Cut off the wire
and secure the end firmly. Push the posy into the posy
frill and bind the stems with gutta percha. Add
ribbon bows at the base of the frill, then glue a few
groups of cloves in the posy.

CHRISTENING POT POURRI

Another idea for a christening is a pot pourri that will
continue the theme of the language of flowers.
Alchemilla (lady's mantle) means protection, aniseed
means indulgence, daisies mean innocence and
beauty, lemon balm (balm) means longevity, heather
means protection, marjoram means health and
happiness, rosebuds mean pure and lovely and allspice
berries mean precious.

15 ml (1 tbsp) dried alchemilla (lady's mantle) sprigs

15 ml (1 tbsp) dried aniseed leaves

15 ml (1 tbsp) dried daisy heads

15 ml (1 tbsp) dried lemon balm (balm)

15 ml (1 tbsp) dried heather

15 ml (1 tbsp) dried marjoram

15 ml (1 tbsp) dried rosebuds

15 ml (1 tbsp) allspice berries

10 ml (2 tsp) powdered orris root

5 ml (1 tsp) perfume or essential oil

Place all the dry ingredients in a large ceramic or
glass bowl and stir them thoroughly with a metal
spoon. Add the perfume or essential oil of your choice
– I used honeysuckle, which means devoted affection
or bonds of love – and stir again. Tip the mixture into
a large plastic bag without any holes, tie the top
securely and leave in a warm airy place for a couple of
weeks, shaking it whenever you remember to do so.
When it is ready, turn it out into a suitable container
– I used a small basket.

134

CHRISTMAS WITH HERBS AND SPICES

♣

Christmas is a busy time for any family, but preparing for it can be just as much fun as the event itself. I always enjoy making the decorations, which I think are a very important part of the celebrations. One of the big bonuses about using dried flowers and herbs in your decorations is that they can be prepared several days or weeks in advance, so are one thing less to worry about in the inevitable last-minute panic. Herbs lend a special aroma to Christmas decorations and the spicy smells of cinnamon and star anise, nutmeg and ginger are memories that stay forever; the smells of Christmas are just as important as the flavours and sights.

RUDOLPH'S NOSEBAG POT POURRI

A Christmassy or festive pot pourri is a wonderful way to add a special aroma to the air and to greet visitors when they arrive. The pot pourri that I like best for Christmas is one that I christened Rudolph's Nosebag, mainly because many of the ingredients might easily be found in his nosebag and also because I think the dried ginger roots look rather like tiny antlers! Pot pourri is very simple to make and, as this recipe includes orange peel (which you can dry out in a low oven) and pine cones, both of which soak up the essential oils and retain their scent well, you can miss out the orris root if you can't find any.

If you have plenty of time before Christmas, it is a lovely idea to make your own wrapping papers and decorate your gifts with sprigs of herbs or bundles of spices.

———— • ————

This recipe makes enough pot pourri to fill quite a large basket.

40-50 small to medium-sized pine cones
2 handfuls chopped dried orange peel
2 handfuls dried apple slices
2 handfuls dried red rose petals
2 handfuls dried nigella seed heads (either gilded or plain)
10-15 cinnamon sticks broken in half
20 pieces dried root ginger
25 ml (5 tsp) essential or perfume oils
10 ml (2 tsp) powdered orris root (optional)
dried whole red roses to decorate the top of the pot pourri

I think the best essential oils for Christmas pot pourris are cinnamon, cranberry, orange, ginger and apple. If you have a selection of these oils you might like to use 5 ml (1 tsp) of each of them, or you could buy a perfume oil (in other words, a ready-mixed blend) that smells suitably fruity and Christmassy. Take the pine cones and drop oil on to each one in turn. This takes some time but it is the best way of ensuring each pine cone is impregnated with the oil because if you just tip the oil over the pile of cones the top ones will soak it all up and the bottom ones will remain unscented. Place all the ingredients, except for the dried red roses, in a large ceramic or glass mixing bowl and stir well with a metal spoon, then tip the mixture into a large plastic bag without any holes, give it a good shake and secure the top of the bag tightly. Leave it to mature for at least 10 days in a warm airy place, shaking it occasionally. When it is ready, tip it into your chosen basket (which you can either leave plain or decorate with flowers and spices) and arrange the dried whole roses on top.

CHRISTMAS TOPIARY TREE

Providing a warm welcome for your guests is important at any time of year – first impressions matter and, even if your visitor is an old friend, it is still nice for him or her to be greeted, especially during the festive season, by a lovely flower arrangement or scented bowl of pine cones. A flower arrangement in the hallway is a cheering sight for arriving guests and sets the tone for a successful visit, and if you choose a dried arrangement you can make it long before you have to worry about food shopping or tidying the house, and can just produce it once all the other chores are out of the way. A basket of flowers always looks delightful but, as a change, a topiary tree can provide a good talking point and, once you have made the base, can be used over and over again

No matter how organized you are, the Christmas season will inevitably mean a lot more work, so the time you allot for making the decorations must be used to the full. One of the best short cuts when making Christmas arrangements and decorations is to use plenty of blue spruce in your work. It is very attractive, has a very Christmassy feel to it, is bulky and fills arrangements, trees and other decorations much quicker than anything else I know!

To make this topiary tree in as little time as possible, I used blue spruce, good-quality *Limonium dumosa* (statice or sea lavender), sticks of cinnamon, gilded wheat, pine cones, ribbon and fabric-covered parcels, which I found sold in a string for decorating Christmas trees. You will also need a terracotta flower-pot or other container for the base, three-quarters filled with cement and with a 46-cm (18-in) long stick set in the centre of the cement. You will also need a 9-cm (3½-in) ball of dried flower foam, about half a rectangular block of it, some heavy-gauge florist's wire and a hot glue gun.

Assuming you are making a fairly small tree, you will need roughly two large branches of blue spruce. Cut up each branch to make pieces about 7.5 cm (3 in) long, then pull the needles off the base of each stalk to make stems. Cut up about a third of a bunch of statice into similar sized lengths and cut or carefully break the cinnamon sticks in half. Using about half a bunch of gilded wheat, cut the stems to the same length as the spruce and statice. Using

———— · ————

If you've ever wondered what Rudolph has in his nosebag,
this pot pourri could give you a clue – or so I think,
anyway! The gilded nigella seed heads look very festive.

heavy-gauge florist's wire, wrap a piece around the bottom end of each pine cone, between the scales and the body of the cone, twist it firmly to hold it in place then bend the leg of the wire so it sticks out like a stalk (stem). The parcels I bought were covered pieces of polystyrene; if you can't find any in the shops you can make your own by covering small cubes of dried flower foam with paper or fabric. Buy or make the parcels you want – you will probably need about 30 or so – and push one end of a piece of the heavy-gauge wire into the base of each parcel so it can be pushed into the tree.

Impale the ball of foam on the top of the stick and push it down until the top of the stick is about halfway through the foam. Then glue pieces of foam, cut from the rectangular block, on to the cement in the base until the foam is level with the rim of the container or flowerpot. Stick some of the pieces of spruce into the foam around the base to make a small arrangement. Make sure you insert pieces at different angles rather than have them all standing up straight like soldiers! Then cover the foam ball with more pieces of spruce, keeping an even outline so the ball appears round rather than looking as though it needs a good haircut. When you have a fair covering of spruce you can push some pieces of statice between the spruce for contrast. If you are careful, the ends of the cinnamon sticks can be pushed into the foam but a much easier way to incorporate them into the tree is to use a hot glue gun and stick them on the spruce and statice. Add more of these ingredients to the base so it matches the ball.

Push in the wired pine cones, trimming the wires if necessary to make them the right length to maintain the spherical shape. Push some into the base too. Then add some parcels, remembering to push them into the base as well as the top. An alternative idea would be to keep the top plain with spruce and a few dried flowers, and only attach parcels to the base, so they look like presents under the tree. Finally, add some ribbon. You can either arrange it, wired in loops, down the trunk of the tree or stick some smaller wired loops of ribbon over the top of the tree and the base.

If you have covered the foam well with the different ingredients and are pleased with the result, you can put the tree away after Christmas and bring it out again the following year, perhaps just changing some of the decorations.

The alternative Christmas topiary trees were made in just the same way as the main tree, with spruce as the main ingredients. For the larger tree I added *Achillea filipendula* (fernleaf yellow yarrow), salignum cones, gilded poppy heads, some stunning gilded artichoke heads and gold lacy ribbon. For the smaller tree, I used yellow thistle-like heads of *Centaurea macrocephela* (globe centaurea), cinnamon sticks, gilded spider claws, dried pomegranates in the base and red ribbons.

These two trees are alternative ideas for a special Christmas topiary tree. If you made a matching pair they could stand either side of a fireplace.

*If you want to make the Christmas Topiary Tree extra
pretty you can decorate it with candles placed around it, but
do take care not to set the foliage alight.*

CHRISTMAS TABLE ARRANGEMENT

I have used spruce again in this table arrangement, because I really do like it and it can be very effective to have matching decorations sometimes. This centrepiece is mildly scented but not so smelly that you can't taste the food. The scented ingredient in this table decoration is the dried ginger root. The pale creamy colour stands out well against the dark spruce and, thanks to the heat of the candles and the room, the ginger gives off a delicious aroma. You could mix other herbs or spices into the arrangement as well as they all have subtle smells.

To make the arrangement, you will need a cork base – in this case, I used an oval base about 17.5 x 12.5 cm (7 x 5 in) across. You will also need a green frog (a four-pronged plastic device used to fix the foam to the base), a block of dried flower foam, two green and pointed candle-holders made specially to be inserted in flower foam, two candles, a large branch of spruce, some dried blue *Agastache foeniculum* (hyssop), some dried *Achillea ptarmica* (sneezewort), cream broom bloom, dried ginger root, some heavy-gauge wire and ribbon.

Glue the green frog on to the centre of the cork base. Cut the block of flower foam in half widthways, then slice that half into two pieces through the middle. If you use a piece of foam that is too tall you will end up with an arrangement that looks rather like a highly decorative hat or pudding! Push the candle holders into the foam, next to each other, then insert the candles as their height will determine the size and scale of the arrangement. This table centre looks best if one candle is longer than the other (chop a short piece off the bottom of one of them). I have used beeswax candles as I like their texture and the sweet smell they give off while burning.

Candles have a very important part to play at Christmas, so I devised this Christmas table arrangement around two creamy-coloured beeswax candles.

Cut the spruce into smaller pieces, stripping the bottom needles off each stalk (stem). Insert one piece of spruce at each end of the arrangement to determine its length, then put two more pieces in the middle of the other two sides to establish the width (you can make the arrangement oval, round or whichever shape you wish). Then add more pieces, keeping to the basic shape you have made. Cover the foam well with spruce as this will form a large part of the arrangement. Do not have long pieces of spruce sticking up near the candles as they could be a fire hazard and might spoil what was otherwise a very successful evening!

When the shape and size of the arrangement is to your liking, add some pieces of the agastache, which has a minty/aniseed smell. The flowers are pointed, so make a good contrast to the softer spruce. Then add some of the dried achillea – I used some that had been dyed a soft lavender but it would look just as attractive in its natural brilliant white. Add some cream broom bloom to echo the creamy colour of the candles. Finally, twist some heavy-gauge wire around some pieces of ginger root and position them throughout the arrangement.

I add ribbon at every available opportunity, and in this case used a burgundy and hunter green tartan ribbon. I wired bunches of the ribbons into loops with fairly long streamers and added them to each end of the arrangement. Finally, keep an eye on the candles when they are lit and have a further supply close to hand when they start to burn down near the decorations or spruce, to ensure no accidents occur.

CINNAMON AND PINE CONE DECORATIONS

These decorations are very simple to make and, if you have children old enough to use a hot glue gun under supervision, you could try having an afternoon when the whole family makes these decorations. The hot glue gun does burn easily and I would not let a child under the age of twelve use one unless they chose where they wanted the glue to go and I squirted it on for them. You can buy a glue gun that melts glue at a much cooler temperature than ordinary hot glue guns and this would be far more suitable for use by

children. Even so, they should still be supervised very carefully as burns can be very painful and sometimes take a long time to heal, which would be no fun at Christmas.

You will need some very large pine cones (I had to buy mine), cinnamon sticks, various dried herbs and flowers, some ribbon, reel wire and the hot glue gun. To make a cinnamon stick decoration, wire or glue the sticks together in bundles of five and tie a ribbon around them in a bow. Decorate the bow with small sprigs of dried herbs and flowers, fixing them in place with small dabs of glue.

For the pine cone, glue a loop of ribbon to the flat end of the cone, then glue on some pieces of spruce, spices, flowers, herbs or even tiny Christmas ornaments. If you wish, you can add a couple of drops of a suitable essential oil to each pine cone to make it thoroughly festive.

All the family can join in making these Cinnamon and Pine Cone Decorations, although you may have to do all the glueing if young children are involved.

SUPPLIERS

Flower arranging specialists, mail order service

The Diddy Box
132-4 Belmont Road
Astley Bridge
Bolton
Lancashire
BL1 7AN

Dried flowers and herbs by mail order and in their shop, which is open on Saturdays only

The Hop Shop
Castle Farm
Shoreham
Sevenoaks
Kent
TN14 7UB

Lavender products; I particularly recommend their oils and beauty products

Jersey Lavender
Rue du Pont Marquet
St Brelade
Jersey
Channel Islands

Lavender products and gifts

Norfolk Lavender Ltd
Caley Mill
Heacham
Kings Lynn
Norfolk
PE31 7JE

Aromatherapy products by mail order

Shirley Price
Wesley House
Stockwell Head
Hinkley
Leicestershire
LE10 1RD

Pressed flower components and details of courses on many dried flower, herb and cookery-related subjects

Joanna Sheen Ltd
PO Box 52
Newton Abott
Devon
TQ12 4YF

Perfume bottles and other lovely glassware in their factory shop

Teign Valley Glass
The Old Potteries
Bovey Tracey
Devon

Aromatherapy products by mail order

The Tisserand Institute
PO Box 746
Hove
East Sussex
BN17 7LR

Many good books have been published on the subject of aromatherapy but I particularly recommend the following:

Aromatherapy for Common Ailments,
Shirley Price, Gaia Books Ltd, 1991

The Art of Aromatherapy,
Robert Tisserand, CW Daniel Co Ltd, 1977

The Aromatherapy Handbook,
Danièle Ryman, CW Daniel Co Ltd, 1989

INDEX